CUT THE CRAP KITCHEN - COSTA RICA

CUT THE
CRAP
—Kitchen—

How-to Cook In Costa Rica
On A Budget

Steve & Nikki Page

Table of Contents

Foreword

It's a proven fact that some of the healthiest cultures around the world share a number of commonalities. These areas, known as Blue Zone (cultures with the largest amount of centenarians) eat healthy foods, stay active, have strong connections and live with a sense of purpose. This life-style sounds like a good recipe for healthy living and one we all should strive for. Unfortunately, many people around the world are sick, over weight and unhealthy, especially in the United States. In fact, over 65% of Americans are overweight and almost half the population has a chronic disease.[1] Those are some staggering statistics. It's no wonder so many people need help with their diets. Many people these days are eating the wrong types of foods. Eating too much processed food, sugar and unhealthy fats can all cause weight gain and illness. Many people turn to fad diets to lose weight, but what people really need is a diet over-haul! Fad diets often only provide a temporary solution. What is needed instead is a life-style change with improved eating habits.

Our society today consumes more processed food containing artificial preservatives and ingredients than real, wholesome foods. This is a problem and where health coaches come in. Health coaches are a wellness authority and provide mentorship and support to clients. Health coaches are on a mission to educate people about eating healthier and you can find them in over 150 countries around the world. As a health coach, I am passionate about helping people learn how to eat healthier and stay active and why I wrote my book, Wholey Cow A Simple Guide To Eating And Living. In my book, I provide 7 guiding principles to help teach people to eat well and live a healthy life-style. I also talk about the importance of getting back to the basics of eating more whole foods to improve our overall health.

In Cut The Crap Kitchen, Steve and Nikki Page share how they did just that after making a move to Costa Rica. Once settled in, they were surprised to find that eating wasn't quite the same in their new home and surroundings. In fact, the food choices were quite limited compared to the vast array they were accustomed to back home in the United States. Many items in Costa Rica are more expensive too, making it a challenge to eat. They discovered quickly they had to change their diet to stay within their budget to live in paradise.

One thing they did to change their diet was to add in more fruit and vegetables. Costa Rica is known for their tropical fruit and abundance of vegetables. They are also a major exporter of pineapples, bananas, melons and some vegetables. Since fruit and vegetables are plentiful and easy to find in Costa Rica, it was relatively easy to add more of them to their daily meals. They also began substituting fruit for snacks instead of unhealthy items such as chips and cookies they were used to eating and in the process literally "cut the crap" out of their diet. Ironically, this is something that health coaches teach their clients and I wrote about in my book. Adding in more fruits and vegetables to your diet and crowding out unhealthy items is important and can make a big difference. Costa Rica has some of the best tasting fruit in the world. And who doesn't like a fresh, juicy pineapple or watermelon? I recently had the opportunity to visit Costa Rica and have to say I had some of the sweetest pineapple I ever tasted. It makes my mouth water just thinking about it.

A second thing Steve and Nikki did to change their diet was to prepare more home-cooked meals. While Costa Rica does have restaurants, they do not have the same amount of establishments per capita or the number of fast food options. In the United States, fast food and processed foods are common place and plentiful, which is one reason why you find so many Americans visiting them. In Costa Rica, dining out is expensive. To make eating more affordable they began to shop for foods that were readily available. Besides fresh produce, what they found was that foods such as rice, beans, eggs and meats were easy to find and fairly inexpensive. They began to make easy recipes with more whole foods and in the process boosted their nutrient intake and in turn their overall health. More home cooked meals are another thing health coaches promote. Making more home cooked meals definitely allows people to make better food choices and to eat healthier.

A third thing Steve and Nikki did to change their diet was to try new things. Costa Rica has a variety of fruits and vegetables that are not common in the United States, or other parts of the world. Not everyone is open to trying something that looks different, or they may never have seen or heard of before. While some fruits and vegetables found in Costa Rica may look odd, their nutrient value is not. Many of these funny looking things such as chayote or mamón chino are loaded with vitamins and minerals, which your body needs and craves. Steve and Nikki share what they learned and offer information about what to try, how certain foods taste and how to eat and cook with them.

They also share how other foods may taste different, as well. In the United States, there are many foods that use GMOs (genetically modified) ingredients making them taste different. In Costa Rica, this is not the case. Most meat and produce is fresh. Farm animals are typically grass-fed, making the meat leaner with a distinct taste. While it may taste a little different, the health benefits to eating more farm fresh foods and less GMO products can affect your overall health and is life changing; another key factor health coaches drive home.

In addition, Steve and Nikki share simple recipes that are easy to make, tasty and nutritious. This book is a good read not only because it shows you how to cook on a budget and save money in your pocket book, but offers a good recipe for getting back to the basics of eating; something we all can benefit from.

Wishing you good health, peace and Pura Vida!

Barbara Rodgers

Author/Certified Integrative Health Coach

Wholey Cow A Simple Guide To Eating And Living

www.barbararodgersonline.com

Source:

[1]"Overweight and Obesity Statistics." National Institutes of Health. U.S. Department of Health and Human Services, n.d. Web. 16 Jan. 2017.

Introduction

Disclosure

Cut the Crap Kitchen is based on our cooking and shopping experiences with some additional research added in. We must disclose that we are not professional chefs, nutrition experts, or doctors, however we have provided insights from a few professionals. Please understand that we are common people who feel that our experiences have yielded some educational understanding about how to shop and cook on a budget in the paradise known as Costa Rica. This book is not necessarily an instruction manual of what you should eat, but rather an overview of what we have found to be some of our favorite foods to prepare and eat; as well as how changing our eating habits has had an impact on our health.

Because we are from the United States, the way we report our experiences will have the perspective of someone coming from the U.S., such as our use of U.S. dollars, the difference in produce available, and the local customs that differ from what we are accustomed to. Understandably, our past lives are the lenses we look through as we discover the differences in our current environment. These understandings of how our current situations differ from our previous lives are where we have found the value and interest that we wish to share with others who may struggle with adapting to life in Central America, especially in regards to what to eat.

Our recommendations for products and services are based on our personal experiences, and we have included hyperlinks for those products, businesses and organizations websites when available.

Who Are Steve and Nikki?

We are a couple in our mid 40s who have one sixteen-year-old daughter at home. In addition, we have two adult daughters and an adult son who live in the United States. We currently live in Tamarindo, Costa Rica, which is where we have called home for nearly four years. We have explored much of the country, from the Nicaraguan border to the Osa Peninsula and Jaco to Limon. We chose the Tamarindo area because of its beautiful beaches and large expat community, which we felt was the key to a smooth transition during our first couple years and are still searching for a better place in Costa Rica to call home.

Why Did We Write This Book?

This book is in response to a large number of requests for advise on how to prepare meals and snacks with produce and products that are different from what many are used to. The fruits and vegetables that are common and available in Central America, especially Costa Rica, differ from those prevalent in places such as our previous home in Colorado, U.S.A. In addition, many of the foods we used to consume in the United States are considerably more expensive in Costa Rica due to import fees. As such, we were forced to change our diet in order to stay within our budget. If we continued to eat the processed foods we had grown accustomed to, or eat at restaurants everyday, we would have gone broke in a hurry. The answer was to learn to shop for and cook more local cuisine with our own gringo flare.

In the process of finding a way to keep our grocery bill within budget, we were able to reap incredible health benefits that we contribute for the most part to our change in diet. Every member of our home has lost weight in the form of body fat. Our skin and hair are more vibrant and smooth. Our immune systems too, have gained a strength we have not experienced before. We also have enjoyed less illness, more strength, and more energy. These are just a few of the changes we have experienced, as we altered the foods we were consuming.

We were never health nuts and still have major sweet tooths. We enjoy our desserts and fried foods as much as the next guy. The difference is these types of foods have become exceptions and not the rule. Trading cookies and chips for fruits and other healthy snacks are major contributing factors. Eating home cooked meals instead of microwave dinners and fast food have increased our nutrient intake and reduced our fat intake. Don't get us wrong, the change was not voluntary, but we could not be happier with the results.

To be honest, if we were still in the United States, we would be hitting up the drive through on our way home from work, or popping a preprepared meal into the microwave. Why?...Because it is fast, convenient, and usually cheaper than preparing food ourselves. In the U.S., it is an option of pay now (preparation time and increased costs) or pay later (overall health/lifestyle and medical care). But, here in Costa Rica, we don't have the fast food options in our region and the frozen food isle contains some of the most expensive choices in the store. We unintentionally traded convenience and time, for quality, nutrition, and health.

Note: Additional color photos can be viewed on our website at:

https://cutthecrapcostarica.com/kitchen-slideshows-shopping-options/

&

https://cutthecrapcostarica.com/kitchen-slideshows-recipes-produce/

Products In Costa Rica

Costa Rica manufactures very few products and imports the vast majority. With this in mind, it is understandable the cost of most goods is high due to basic supply and demand principles. Costa Rica's population is 4.9 million (roughly the same as the state of Alabama), which is only 1.5% of the 325.7 million people of the United States. The consumer pool is much smaller, so businesses must select only those items they know will sell. Because of these factors and others, the diversity of product options is less than in the United States.

Depending on the region of Costa Rica you find yourself in, shopping options can vary drastically. As previously mentioned, we live in Tamarindo, which is a growing community. In the short time we have lived in the area, there have been a number of businesses that have opened and provide new sources for the things we need.

One example is the recent opening of Maxi Pali, which is basically a mini Walmart, as it is owned by the global retail giant. This has given us access to foods, cooking supplies, and other household items that when we first arrived, required a forty-five minute drive to Santa Cruz. The nearest Walmart was in San Jose, a five hour drive, until they opened the store in Liberia in 2017, about one hour away. While we now have closer access to Walmart and its little brothers, selection is still quite limited on certain products and others are still expensive imports.

Everywhere we have lived has been furnished, but not all of them had full appliances. Since we do more cooking at home now, we have started to bring more things that have to do with the kitchen and cooking back from the U.S. Items like hand mixers, electric pressure cookers, and hot water kettles. All of these things are higher priced in the beach area, so every time we go back to the United States, we try to throw a small appliance in our suitcase. If you are not yet currently living in the country, we suggest brining the small appliances you feel you will need. Worst-case scenario, you can sell them and get your money back when you get here.

TIP: Our number one recommended small appliance is an electric pressure cooker. (See the Recommended Tools & Appliances section)

Our experience has taught us to be open to trying new fruits, vegetables, fish, and new ways of preparing foods. We have had to change our thinking to stop saying, "This is way more expensive than in the States," because it doesn't matter what it costs in the U.S. Our present reality is we are in Costa Rica, so the value or cost of an item is based on our current economy. This mindset is how we decide what is worth throwing in our suitcases, what we can live without, and what we are willing to pay more for than we did in the past.

For example, our son just came for a visit and brought peanut butter. In the States, peanut butter was a major staple for our family, and we consumed it at a rate of about a large jar a week. Although peanut butter is available at most stores, it has a very high markup, making it a specialty item for us.

While you are able to buy it in bulk in San Jose or Liberia at a cheaper price, it's still very expensive. When we first got here, several months passed until we had a visitor bring some with them. Now we try to have a couple jars put in each suitcase that's brought down. It's now a treat not a staple and in our house. This experience helped us appreciate the small things in life, like a peanut butter and jelly sandwich.

Since living in Costa Rica, our eyes have really been opened to food. Most fruits and vegetables native to Costa Rica are a stark contrast to what we were used to in the United States. Even common things like watermelon and pineapple taste considerably different. Meat such as chicken, pork and fish all have a different taste, as well. Costa Rica has less GMO crops, and most animals are free range. These along with other food production practices affect the taste.

There seems to be a stronger emphasis on fresh foods like bread and produce than processed packaged foods. With all these differences, our family has enjoyed trying new meals and unusual fruits and vegetables. Many food options look very strange or unappetizing, but are quite delicious. Although Costa Rica is not known for great cuisine, we have certainly broadened our tastes and have enjoyed more fresh fruit and vegetables than we used to.

Shopping Options

Mini Super

Throughout Costa Rica, "mini super" shops are like convenience stores. These shops can be part of people's homes, or in commercial complexes. The further away from tourist areas, the more often they are part of a family's porch, rather than their own entity. Most of the mini supers have eggs, milk, drinks, liquor, and dry goods (bread, beans, rice, cereal, etc.). You can likely find some cheese and/or baked goods, such as empanadas and sweet breads, made by local families, as well. As in other countries, you pay for the convenience of the location of these shops, so the prices can be considerably higher than the larger mercados (markets).

Grocery Store/Supermercado

In cities and tourist areas, large grocery stores not only stock produce, deli, and bakery items, but also stock a lot of the same products you would find in the U.S. (You can get your bag of Cheetos to go with your Pillsbury cake mix.) Grocery stores in Costa Rica offer the staples you need and may also provide some comforts of home, albeit at a price. (Check the section on Prices to see what items may be expensive or difficult to find.)

Some stores offer sale days where they place several items on sale every week. Each store has something different to offer, and you may pay a bit more for items in a cleaner and more modern store.

Location is also a major factor in price. If the mercado is in the center of town within walking distance to many people, the prices may be slightly higher.

If you have done some research and heard about the Walmarts in Costa Rica, you should throttle your expectations.

Yes, there are Walmarts in a couple of large cities, but the stores are not nearly as large, nor do they have the variety or quality of products compared to the stores in the United States. You may be able to find some items cheaper at Walmart than in smaller towns, but often the savings and selection are not worth the time and gas money.

Butcher Shop - Carnicería

Although you can purchase meat and poultry at the grocery stores and some mini supers, another option is to buy from the local butcher shop called a carnicería in Spanish. We prefer the meat from <u>Centro De Carnes Villa Mar</u>, the carnicería in the nearby village of Villareal. The meat has a slightly different taste than that of the United States and may take some getting used to. The meat is generally leaner, so it doesn't cook quite the same as what we were accustomed to. (This became very evident when we tried making hamburgers! They always require eggs and crackers to hold form.) Canicerías have proven to have low prices compared to the other stores, as well. We find ourselves eating more chicken than beef, or pork simply because it tastes great. Not only does chicken taste great, but our doctors have recommended removing red meat from our

diet.

Fish Options

Grocery Stores

Most larger grocery stores have a selection of fresh fish and seafood. The fish may be prepackaged in a refrigerated area or on ice behind a counter depending on the size of the store. That means that depending on where you live and which store you shop at will determine the freshness of the fish available. The fish comes from the same processing centers as the fish markets in most cases. Unless on sale, the grocery stores are one of the more expensive options.

Fish Markets

In most larger towns you can find a fish market. These markets offer fish that was caught with commercial fishing boats. In Costa Rica the commercial fishing boats. You can find a variety of fish such as mahi-mahi (known locally as dorado), tuna, red snapper, and shrimp to name a few. The quality and selection will vary depending on the size of the community. Often these markets offer fish that has been frozen and packaged. Unless you live near a fishing port, the fish markets may not be the freshest option.

Fish Truck

A common way to get fish in Costa Rica is from a fish truck. These are the same trucks that deliver to restaurants. If you call them, they will email you a menu, or give you the prices over the phone. You can place your order by calling the office the day prior and they will deliver the fish to you. The fish trucks only deliver to certain towns on certain days of the week, so you need to plan ahead. If you do not live in the center of town you may need to meet them at a local restaurant or other central location. Again the fish provided by the trucks is usually frozen and packaged, so freshness may be a concern.

Local Fisherman

If you live near the coast or a large river, you can purchase fish from local fisherman. Most do not have a business license or permit of any kind, so it is a bit of an "under the table" type arrangement. We have tried this method before. We called a number to a fisherman that our Tico friend knew. The fisherman brought fresh fish right to (our) front door. They even cleaned them. Mahi-mahi and red snapper cost us around $13 (pictured in the slideshow above). This is probably one of the freshest options for fish.

Sportfishing Tour

Another option for getting fresh fish is to take a sport fishing tour and hook a fish yourself. The boat provides the tackle and expertise, you provide the sweat and good times. We (recommend) you get a fishing license if you choose this option. This is probably the most expensive way to enjoy fish in Costa Rica, but the experience and memories may make up for it. Usually you keep what you catch, so this is definitely a fresh fish option. Some boats offer to prepare the fish for you as well.

Spearfishing

Last, of all, there is a spearfishing option, which is one of the cheapest options. If you are a good swimmer and enjoy snorkeling and freediving, this option may be perfect for you. It may, however, take some practice and research about the local waters to bring home your dinner though. Spearfishing is a bit more like hunting than fishing. Unlike standard fishing, you are able to see and at times track your prey instead of simply throwing a line in the water and hoping there is something good on the other end. This is how our friend Mike acquires the fish he serves at his restaurant, Jalapeño's, which is located in Playa Negra.

Ferias and Fruit Stands

For produce, there is the option of the ferias and fruit stands. Since they specialize in produce, ferias are generally a bit cheaper than supermercados. Ferias have two forms; some are similar to farmers markets where various farmers and vendors sell produce and goods, while others are a single owner or company selling the produce of many farms. Fruit stands, on the other had, are generally a single private owner selling items from their own farm. We have a company owned feria in nearby Villareal that is open every day, but most ferias are only open once, or twice a week. Tamarindo has a feria that is open on Saturday mornings, where local farmers and merchants bring produce and goods to sell. There are several fruit stands both in towns and along the roads throughout the area. Most weeks we choose to get our produce from the feria called Come Fruta in Villareal, as it seems to be fresh, good quality, and a low price. That being said, pricing is typically slightly higher on Sundays and Mondays.

Pickup Truck Produce

When the farmers or families with fruit trees harvest, they often load the back of a pickup with their produce and park on the side of the road in the middle of town. Many of our friends have commented that the best watermelon and pineapple they have ever eaten was off a pickup truck in Costa Rica. This is often a great way to purchase unique produce at a good price by cutting out the middlemen. Our family recommends you try some Mamón Chinos and Maracuyá. Don't be (afraid) of the spiky appearance, or slimy texture. Just open your mouth and let your taste buds enjoy the tropical goodness.

We have learned to treat the fruit trucks, stands, and ferias like we used to treat the fast food stores in the states. Instead of pulling through and grabbing a cheap hamburger and fries, we now pull through and grab a piece of fresh fruit. This has not only saved in the pocketbook, but has given us all more energy.

Kitchen Goods

To purchase things like small kitchen appliances, pots and pans, silverware, dishes, plastic containers, etc., we recommend visiting stores like Walmart, Maxi Pali, or Mundo Magico, which are in located in larger towns. Many towns have smaller stores simply known as "plastic stores." The smaller stores will not have the appliances, but should carry things such as utensils, plastic wrap and containers. The prices are usually slightly higher than the larger stores, but what you save in gas when purchasing a few items, makes up for it.

For major kitchen appliances like ovens, microwaves, and small kitchen appliances, there are Coopeguanacaste and Gollo stores in many towns throughout the area. Remember these items will cost more than in the States, so you may want to pack small appliances like blenders and juicers in your luggage.

Recommended Tools and Appliances

As we mentioned earlier, most products are expensive in Costa Rica, due to import fees. With that in mind, we have provided a few items that we use on a regular basis below. These items are the types of things you should consider putting in your luggage to bring from your home country, as they most likely will be much cheaper there. To save you time, links to these items can be found on our website at:

https://cutthecrapcostarica.com/kitchen/recommended-products/

Apron

Every cook knows that food is messy. You don't have time to change clothes to make a quick snack or prepare tonight's dinner. Throwing on an apron takes a few seconds, but can save you hours in trying to get that stain out of your favorite shirt, or pair of pants. Inevitably, your spouse or child will fly into the kitchen or bump you as you are slicing a dragon fruit or pouring your cup of coffee. Save yourself the time and energy of stain-fighting by getting an apron.

Measuring Cups & Spoons

We were surprised we had difficulty finding measuring cups and spoons in Costa Rica. It seems that most Ticos cook with pinches, dashes, and regular cups for measurement. Nowadays you can find some measuring tools at the major supermercados, or department stores, but if you prefer a specific style, it is best to bring them with you, as the selection is definitely limited.

Stainless Steel Metal Straw

Why not make your drinks taste better and save the planet at the same time? We all know that drinks (especially mixed drinks) taste better through a straw. These stainless steel metal straws work great for accessing coconut water from a fresh pipa fria (cold coconut), too. Because they are metal, it's easy to puncture carpels (holes), without the need of a knife or machete. They also work great for both 30oz and 20oz Tumblers, Cups, and Mugs.

Pineapple Slicer

Sure you can always simply slice the pineapple with a knife, but sometimes switching it up and creating rings can change the feel of the dish. Our experience has been, changing the shape makes the pineapple more appealing and taste better. This pineapple slicer provides a quick way to enjoy a tasty treat.

Cutting Board

Cutting boards are a must in every kitchen. Whether chopping up a piece of fruit for a quick snack or preparing a meal for an army, cutting boards make the process of cutting and chopping easier. It's nice to have multiple sized cutting boards too. Who wants to wash your cutting board before chopping or mincing your next item if you don't have to. Small cutting boards work great for a number of fruits too. We prefer the type with a juice groove, especially for watermelon and other high liquid items. Make sure you have a few cutting boards on hand for your favorite fruits and vegetables.

Knife Set

Did you know the knife is the number one tool for any kitchen? That's right! It doesn't matter if you are an amateur or a professional cook, this tool is used more than any other. If you watch the really good chefs, you will notice the importance they put on their knives. Knives are an investment. After all, they are your primary kitchen tool and are used to prepare a variety of foods. That's why it's important to have sharp, good-quality knives. Knives can be found at supermercados or department stores, but if you prefer a specific style, it is best to bring them with you. The selection is definitely limited in Costa Rica unless you travel to the San Jose or Liberia. If you don't want to make the trip, you may want to consider bringing a good quality set with you.

Silicon Fruit & Veggie Storage

Want a quick and easy way to store your cut fruit and vegetables? Give these silicone fruit and veggie storage savers a try. These simple little food savers come in handy and are quick and easy to use. Simply slide the silicone on the cut end of tomato, onion, cucumber...whatever. They are dishwasher safe and you don't have to waste any time looking for a missing lid for a container. If you don't have a dishwasher, they are easy to hand-wash too. They are also easy to store and nest together, so they don't take up much cupboard space. In addition, they are color coded, so you can quickly identify the size you want.

Banjo or Mandolin Slicer

Aside from our knives, our slicer is the next most used tool in our kitchen. It is much faster and more precise than hand slicing. We can churn out a quick slaw salad in a matter of a few short minutes thanks to this appliance. Make sure you look for one with the slicing guard to help protect your fingers, as these babies are sharp! The cheap version is very common in Costa Rica, but you may want to consider an upgrade if you enjoy sliced fruits and vegetables like us.

Hot Water Kettle

After over three years of tests and trials, we have concluded that the Hot Water Kettle is the way to make water for coffee in Costa Rica. We have tried standard coffee pots and three broke in a single year. Not to mention the coffee wasn't as good. There are other ways to heat water, but the electric kettle is the fastest and most energy efficient solution we have found. Hot water kettles are cheap and have a multitude of uses, from making hot beverages to heating up water for instant soups etc. We recommend removing any excess water immediately following use and washing regularly. The minerals in the local water can cause a nasty buildup. Cleaning the pot regularly with vinegar has really helped us keep our kettle in good shape.

Immersion Blender

Standard Blenders can sometimes be a big pain to maintain and wash. Luckily we found an immersion blender that works great for single serving smoothies and cocktails. This immersion blender works great for frozen fruit drinks, as well as delicious soups and sauces. Cleanup is as simple as mixing a glass of soapy water and it works great to clean both the mixer and the glass. It also doesn't take up very much storage space, and makes a great addition to any kitchen.

Hand Mixer

No kitchen is complete without a hand mixer. Whether mixing up a batch of banana pancakes or whipping up some frosting for a cake, a hand mixer is a must. Unfortunately, many rentals in Costa Rica fail to offer this simple appliance. While you can always mix your cake, cookies, or gravy by hand, hand mixers save time and typically blend food items together better. Like other appliances in Costa Rica, selection, and options are limited. In addition, prices may be more than you want to pay, so we recommend bringing a hand-mixer with you.

Costa Rica Coffee Maker

COFFEE! Some call it the nectar of life. I like to call it my "go juice". Regardless of what you call it, Costa Rica has some of the best coffee in the world. If you want to really experience Costa Rican coffee the traditional way, however, you need a Costa Rican Coffee Maker. The pour-over sock method creates the perfect aromatic treasure of rich flavor and bold presence. This coffee maker is easy to fold up and take on the go when you travel and will allow you to experience the best coffee wherever you go. Replacement socks are easy to find throughout Costa Rica or can be ordered online.

Electric Pressure Cooker / Slow Cooker

OUR NUMBER ONE BRING WITH YOU ITEM!!!

The electric pressure cooker, a slow cooker is the most important appliance for eating on a budget. In fact, we prepare the majority of our meals with this one appliance. It is extremely versatile and a great energy saver too. Not only does it take much less electricity to cook items like beans and soups, but it also puts out much less heat than an oven, which saves on air conditioning costs. This electric pressure cooker is great for meats, vegetables, grains, soups, and so much more. It is a great addition to any kitchen.

Costa Rica Pricing

Exchange Rate

While you might be used to using dollars, or some other currency for money, the colón is the currency used in Costa Rica. The exchange rate varies, but when this book was written, the rate was somewhere around 600 colones to the United States dollar. Realizing that a single colón is worth a fraction of a penny, it can make the conversion seem like a daunting task. We will try to explain the process in a simple way, to help it make sense.

When purchasing items from street vendors, ferias, and small shops, they generally use a 500 to 1 ratio, making for easier math. Using this ratio, you can take the price in colones, double it, and then move the decimal three places to get the dollar amount. For example, if a watermelon costs 4,000 colones (pronounced 4 mil because mil means thousand in Spanish), you would double it (8,000) then move the decimal to get the U.S. equivalent of $8.00 (4000≈8). Converting can get confusing when dealing with larger amounts, but the same principle applies. If a house costs 175,000,000 colones, it would be around $350,000 USD using the 500/1 ratio. The opposite conversion is relatively easy, as well. For example, if we have $15 in our pocket, the equivalent is 7,500 colones.

Of course, when using the 500/1 ratio, you are losing about 17¢ per dollar, depending on the exchange rate. This is not too much of an issue for small purchases, such as a single piece of fruit that is under $1; however, the example of the house would cost you $291,666 if you use a ratio of 600/1, so you would save over $58,000 by paying in colones or using the proper ratio.

Common Costa Rican Denominations & Approximate U.S. Value.

Table 1 - Basic Currency Conversion

Coins	600/1	500/1
₡20	$0.03	$0.05
₡50	$0.08	$0.10
₡100	$0.17	$0.20
₡500	$0.83	$1.00
Paper		
₡1000	$1.66	$2.00
₡2000	$3.32	$4.00
₡5000	$8.31	$10.00
₡10000	$16.61	$20.00
₡20000	$33.22	$40.00

The bottom line is that whatever currency the item is listed in, is usually the most cost-effective way to pay. There are fees and inconvenience to exchanging money that must be taken into consideration, so if you are planning on spending a considerable amount of time in Costa Rica, it is worth using the local currency as much as possible.

Prices

Prices on items in Costa Rica are going to be in local currency (Colones – ₡) and use the metric unit of measure. For those coming from the U.S., this means a double conversion of a unit of measure and currency. Here are a few formulas to help calculate the conversions.

Items in Kilos vs. Pounds — Produce & deli products are sold in kilograms (2.2 pounds. per kilo or .454 kilo per pound).

Equation 1 - Colones Per Kilograms to Dollar per Pound

$$\frac{₡Price}{kilograms} * \frac{1\,(kilo)}{2.2\,(pounds)} * \frac{\$1}{₡600}$$

Example: One kilo of chicken breast costs ₡3,900. If we place that price in the equation, we get the following:

*Exchange rate of ₡600=$1, you will need to update with the current exchange rate.

$$\frac{₡3900}{1\,(kilo)} * \frac{1(kilo)}{2.2\,(pounds)} * \frac{\$1}{₡600} = \frac{3900}{1320} = \text{Chicken breast costs \$2.95 per pound}$$

Items in Liters vs. Gallons — Liquid is sold in liters (3.79 liters per gallon or .264 gallons per liter)

Formula ₡ per L to $ per Gal.:

Equation 2 - Liters per Colones to Gallons per Dollar

$$\frac{₡Price}{liters} * \frac{1(liters)}{.264\ (gallons)} * \frac{\$1}{₡600}$$

Example: One liter of orange juice costs ₡700. If we place that price in the equation, we get the following:

*Exchange rate of ₡600=$1, you will need to update with the current exchange rate for accuracy. See the section on Exchange Rate..

$$\frac{₡700}{(liters)} * \frac{1(liters)}{.264\ (gallons)} * \frac{\$1}{₡600} = \frac{700}{158.4} = Orange\ Juice\ costs\ \$4.42\ per\ gallon.$$

Although prices for goods are constantly changing, we thought it might be helpful to include a snapshot of the current prices in the area. Of course, by the time anyone actually gets here, the market may have fluctuated and the following charts won't be completely accurate, but hopefully they will give you a point of reference.

Table 2 - Prices

General Grocery

INGREDIENT	Amount	PRICE ¢ - Colones	PRICE $ -Dollars	SERVING/ AMT	SERVING PRICE ¢	SERVING PRICE $
Baking Powder - Escazu	100g	CRC 695.00	$1.16	1 tsp	CRC 33.13	$0.06
Baking Soda - Arm & Hammer	1lb / 454g	CRC 915.00	$1.53	1 tsp	CRC 28.82	$0.05
Basil Ground (21.3g)	1 Bottle	CRC 1,365.00	$2.28	1 tsp.	CRC 90.72	$0.15
Bay Leaf (5.67g)	1 Bag	CRC 740.00	$1.23	2 Leaves	CRC 78.31	$0.13
Beans Black	Kilo	CRC 1,145.00	$1.91	1 Cup	CRC 229.00	$0.38
Beans Red (800g)	1 Bag	CRC 1,000.00	$1.67	1 Cup	CRC 200.00	$0.33
Beans Refried (795g)	1 Bag	CRC 940.00	$1.57	1/2 Cup	CRC 153.40	$0.26
Black Pepper (Whole with grinder, 63.8g)	1 Bottle	CRC 2,575.00	$4.29	1 tsp.	CRC 92.83	$0.15
Cereal - Fruit Loops 6.3oz / 180g	1 Box	CRC 1,750.00	$2.92	1 Cup	CRC 281.94	$0.47
Cereal - Kellogg's Complete Muesli Almonds 410g / 14.4oz	1 Box	CRC 2,250.00	$3.75	1 Cup	CRC 164.63	$0.27
Cereal - Raisin Bran 18.7oz 530g	1 Box	CRC 4,995.00	$8.33	1 Cup	CRC 250.00	$0.42
Coconut Oil (887ml)	1 Jar	CRC 6,795.00	$11.33	1 Tbsp	CRC 113.25	$0.19
Cumin Ground (56.7g)	1 Bottle	CRC 1,365.00	$2.28	1 Tbsp	CRC 144.42	$0.24
Flour Baking - Gluten Free (1000g)	1 Bag	CRC 3,630.00	$6.05	1/4 Cup	CRC 108.90	$0.18
Flour Coconut - Gluten Free (450g)	1 Box	CRC 3,705.00	$6.18	1/4 Cup	CRC 327.88	$0.55
Flour White Wheat (2500g)	1 Bag	CRC 1,805.00	$3.01	1/4 Cup	CRC 21.66	$0.04
Hot Sauce - Chilero Con Ajo (155g)	1 Jar	CRC 740.00	$1.23	5g	CRC 24.67	$0.04
Jelly (Grape - 300)	1 Bag	CRC 910.00	$1.52	1 Tbsp	CRC 72.80	$0.12
Jelly (Pineapple - 300g)	1 Bag	CRC 695.00	$1.16	1 Tbsp	CRC 46.33	$0.08
Jelly (Strawberry - 300)	1 Bag	CRC 910.00	$1.52	1 Tbsp	CRC 72.80	$0.12

INGREDIENT	Amount	PRICE ¢ - Colones	PRICE $ -Dollars	SERVING/ AMT	SERVING PRICE ¢	SERVING PRICE $
Lizano (400g)	1 Unit	CRC 1,000.00	$1.67	2 tsp.	CRC 28.57	$0.05
Maggi Consomé de pollo Concentrado - Chicken Concentrate (5 pack - 40g)	Pk	CRC 505.00	$0.84	1 Package	CRC 101.00	$0.17
Magi Sopa Criolla Gallina Con Fideos (57g)	Pk	CRC 400.00	$0.67	1/5 Pk	CRC 80.00	$0.13
Mayonnaise (400g/bag, 15g/Tbsp	1 Bag	CRC 1,175.00	$1.96	1 Tbsp	CRC 44.06	$0.07
Mustard (200g)	1 Bag	CRC 1,000.00	$1.67	1 Tbsp	CRC 66.68	$0.11
Oatmeal (400g)	1 Bag	CRC 970.00	$1.62	1 Cup	CRC 242.50	$0.40
Olive Oil - Filippo Berio Extra Virgin	500ml	CRC 4,695.00	$7.83	1 Tbsp	CRC 138.85	$0.23
Oregano (Ground - Serving 14g)	1 Bag	CRC 630.00	$1.05	1 tsp.	CRC 81.00	$0.14
Paprika Ground (28.3g)	Pk	CRC 740.00	$1.23	1 tsp.	CRC 64.75	$0.11
Pasta Linguine (500g)	Pk	CRC 1,025.00	$1.71	55g	CRC 112.75	$0.19
Pasta Shells (8oz / 250g)	Pk	CRC 560.00	$0.93	55g	CRC 124.44	$0.21
Pasta Spaghetti (400g)	Pk	CRC 910.00	$1.52	55g	CRC 130.00	$0.22
Pasta Spaghetti - Gluten Free (250g)	Pk	CRC 2,280.00	$3.80	56g	CRC 506.67	$0.84
Peanut Butter (454g)	Can	CRC 3,745.00	$6.24	2 Tbsp	CRC 296.96	$0.49
Rice Integral 95%	Kilo	CRC 970.00	$1.62	1 Cup	CRC 194.00	$0.32
Rice White 80%	Kilo	CRC 610.00	$1.02	1 Cup	CRC 122.00	$0.20
Rice White 99%	Kilo	CRC 840.00	$1.40	1 Cup	CRC 168.00	$0.28
Rosemary Ground (14.1g)	Pk	CRC 630.00	$1.05	1 tsp.	CRC 53.62	$0.09
Salt (500g)	Pk	CRC 330.00	$0.55	1 tsp.	CRC 3.96	$0.01
Spaghetti Sauce - (Natura's Carne 227g)	Pk	CRC 680.00	$1.13	1 Tbsp	CRC 85.00	$0.14
Sugar - White (2Kg)	Pk	CRC 1,325.00	$2.21	1 tsp.	CRC 0.53	$0.00
Thyme Ground (14.2g)	Pk	CRC 740.00	$1.23	1 tsp.	CRC 59.41	$0.10

Produce

INGREDIENT	Amount	PRICE ¢ - Colones	PRICE $ -Dollars	SERVING/ AMT	SERVING PRICE ¢	SERVING PRICE $
Apple - Fuji (182g)	Kilo	CRC 4,095.00	$6.83	1 Whole	CRC 745.29	$1.24
Apple - Gala (182g)	Kilo	CRC 3,140.00	$5.23	1 Whole	CRC 571.48	$0.95
Apple - Granny Smith (182g)	Kilo	CRC 3,415.00	$5.69	1 Whole	CRC 621.53	$1.04
Avocado (201g)	Kilo	CRC 5,460.00	$9.10	1 Whole	CRC 682.50	$1.14
Banana (medium 118 grams)	Kilo	CRC 710.00	$1.18	1 Whole	CRC 50.00	$0.08
Banana (small 30 grams)	Kilo	CRC 1,200.00	$2.00	1 Whole	CRC 50.00	$0.08
Banana Green	Unit	CRC 50.00	$0.08	1 Whole	CRC 50.00	$0.08
Beans Green	Kilo	CRC 1,440.00	$2.40	1 Cup	CRC 144.00	$0.24
Cabbage Green/White	Kilo	CRC 900.00	$1.50	1 Cup	CRC 63.00	$0.11
Cabbage Red/Purple	Kilo	CRC 950.00	$1.58	1 Cup	CRC 66.50	$0.11
Camote (130g each)	Kilo	CRC 800.00	$1.33	1 Whole	CRC 104.00	$0.17
Carrots (280 g)	Kilo	CRC 650.00	$1.08	1 Whole	CRC 182.00	$0.30
Celery (380g)	Kilo	CRC 1,890.00	$3.15	1 Stalk	CRC 718.20	$1.20
Chayote (203 grams)	Pk 7	CRC 1,000.00	$1.67	1 Whole	CRC 142.86	$0.24
Chives Fresh (60g/3g)	Bundle	CRC 830.00	$1.38	1 Tbsp	CRC 41.50	$0.07
Cilantro (Fresh 60g/.9g)	Bundle	CRC 200.00	$0.33	.5 Tbsp	CRC 47.67	$0.08
Coconuts Meat (5 Cups Shredded)	1 Unit	CRC 333.00	$0.56	1 Whole	CRC 333.00	$0.56
Coconuts Milk (13.5oz)	1 Can	CRC 1,895.00	$3.16	1/4 Cup	CRC 1,139.16	$1.90
Coconuts Water (1 Cup)	1 Unit	CRC 333.00	$0.56	1 Whole	CRC 333.00	$0.56
Cucumber	Kilo	CRC 1,000.00	$1.67	1 Whole	CRC 410.00	$0.68
Eggplant	1 Unit	CRC 600.00	$1.00	1 Whole	CRC 600.00	$1.00
Garlic	Pk 3	CRC 250.00	$0.42	1 Clove	CRC 8.33	$0.01
Granadilla - Passion Fruit	1 Unit	CRC 200.00	$0.33	1 Whole	CRC 200.00	$0.33
Grape - Green Seedless (10 grapes/49g)	Kilo	CRC 6,250.00	$10.42	10 Grapes	CRC 306.36	$0.51
Grape - Red Seedless (10 grapes/49g)	Kilo	CRC 6,250.00	$10.42	10 Grapes	CRC 306.36	$0.51
Grape - Red with Seeds (10 grapes/49g)	Kilo	CRC 3,990.00	$6.65	10 Grapes	CRC 195.51	$0.33

Guanabana - Sour Sop (225g)	Kilo	CRC 2,935.00	$4.89	1 Cup	CRC 660.38	$1.10
Lettuce - American	head	CRC 420.00	$0.70	1 Cup	CRC 84.00	$0.14
Lettuce - Romaine	head	CRC 475.00	$0.79	1 Cup	CRC 95.00	$0.16
Lime - Limon Mandarin (10 count)	1 Bag	CRC 950.00	$1.58	1 Whole	CRC 95.00	$0.16
Mamón Chino - Rambutan (28g)	Kilo	CRC 1,500.00	$2.50	1 Whole	CRC 42.00	$0.07
Mango (336g w/out refuse - 1/2 of fruit)	Kilo	CRC 1,400.00	$2.33	1 Half Fruit	CRC 900.00	$1.50
Maracuyá - Passion Fruit	Kilo	CRC 1,500.00	$2.50	1 Whole	CRC 375.00	$0.63
Melon - Cantaloupe (1 cup/170g)	Kilo	CRC 895.00	$1.49	1 Cup	CRC 152.15	$0.25
Mushrooms (500g/tray, 96g/cup)	1 Tray	CRC 4,180.00	$6.97	1 Cup	CRC 802.56	$1.34
Onion - Small (60 grams)	Kilo	CRC 750.00	$1.25	1 Whole	CRC 45.00	$0.08
Oranges (local - bag of 25)	Pk	CRC 2,365.00	$3.94	1 Whole	CRC 94.60	$0.16
Oregano (Dried - Serving 1g)	30g	CRC 840.00	$1.40	1 tsp.	CRC 28.00	$0.05
Papaya (Serving 145g)	Kilo	CRC 840.00	$1.40	1 Cup	CRC 121.80	$0.20
Pineapple	1 Fruit	CRC 500.00	$0.83	1 Cup	CRC 91.16	$0.15
Plantain (Medium 179g)	Pk 7	CRC 1,000.00	$1.67	1 Whole	CRC 142.86	$0.24
Chips - Plantain Platanos Caribenos (28g)	Pk	CRC 580.00	$0.97	1 Whole	CRC 580.00	$0.97
Chips - Plantain Soldanza Platanos (180g)	Pk	CRC 955.00	$1.59	28g 30 chips	CRC 66.83	$0.11
Potatoes - Red (213g)	Kilo	CRC 1,806.00	$3.01	1 Whole	CRC 384.68	$0.64
Potatoes Yellow Medium (213g)	Kilo	CRC 1,860.00	$3.10	1 Whole	CRC 396.18	$0.66
Potatoes Yellow Small (170g)	Kilo	CRC 1,250.00	$2.08	1 Whole	CRC 212.50	$0.35
Radishes (4-pack Large)	Pk	CRC 600.00	$1.00	1 Whole	CRC 150.00	$0.25
Raspberries (125g/Box)	Pk	CRC 2,645.00	$4.41	10 Raspber-ries/20g	CRC 423.20	$0.71
Strawberries (700g/Box, 144g/cup)	Pk	CRC 5,145.00	$8.58	1 Cup	CRC 1,058.40	$1.76
Sweet Pepper - Chili Dulce (4-pack)	Pk	CRC 1,000.00	$1.67	1 Whole	CRC 250.00	$0.42
Tomato (3.5oz)	Kilo	CRC 750.00	$1.25	1 Whole	CRC 75.00	$0.13
Watermelon	Kilo	CRC 500.00	$0.83	1 Cup	CRC 76.00	$0.13
Yuca (408g)	Kilo	CRC 600.00	$1.00	1 Whole	CRC 244.80	$0.41
Zucchini - Medium (196g)	1 Unit	CRC 600.00	$1.00	1 Whole	CRC 600.00	$1.00

Dairy

INGREDIENT	Amount	PRICE ¢ Colones	PRICE $ Dollars	SERVING/ AMT	SERVING PRICE ¢	SERVING PRICE $
Butter no-salt (4 Sticks)	1 Box	CRC 3,695.00	$6.16	1 Tbsp	CRC 117.86	$0.20
Cheese (Shredded - Crystal Farms 8oz)	1 Bag	CRC 2,995.00	$4.99	1 Cup	CRC 374.38	$0.62
Cheese Slices (Marble Jack - 226g)	Pk 10	CRC 3,530.00	$5.88	1 Slice	CRC 353.00	$0.59
Cream Cheese (650g)	650g	CRC 3,750.00	$6.25	1 Tbsp	CRC 46.16	$0.08
Cream Sweet - Crema Dulce - Blue Box (250ml)	1 Box	CRC 1,195.00	$1.99	1 Tbsp	CRC 74.69	$0.12
Cream Sweet - Crema Dulce Italiana-Green Box (200ml)	1 Box	CRC 865.00	$1.44	100ml	CRC 432.50	$0.72
Egg - Raw	Kilo	CRC 1,710.00	$2.85	1 Whole	CRC 57.00	$0.10
Ice Cream - Dos Piños Vanilla 1028g / 1892ml	1 Tub	CRC 5,375.00	$8.96	1/2 Cup	CRC 335.94	$0.56
Milk 2%	1.8 L	CRC 1,000.00	$1.67	1 Cup	CRC 131.58	$0.22
Sour Cream (Natilla Casera - farmers - 480g)	Pk	CRC 1,100.00	$1.83	1 Tbsp	CRC 35.22	$0.06
Sour Cream (Natilla La Granja Livian - 400g)	Pk	CRC 1,000.00	$1.67	1 Tbsp	CRC 38.45	$0.06
Ice cream Trits - Ice cream Sandwich	Pk	CRC 960.00	$1.60	1 Whole	CRC 960.00	$1.60

Baked Goods

INGREDIENT	Amount	PRICE ¢ Colones	PRICE $ Dollars	SERVING/ AMT	SERVING PRICE ¢	SERVING PRICE $
Bread - Fresh French (10 servings)	1 Loaf	CRC 725.00	$1.21	1 Slice	CRC 72.50	$0.12
Bread (Bimbo White Sandwich)	1 Loaf	CRC 1,500.00	$2.50	1 Slice	CRC 50.00	$0.08
Brownie Mix - Betty Crocker Fudge 8X8 (Makes 20 servings)	1 Box	CRC 1,145.00	$1.91	1 Piece	CRC 57.25	$0.10
Cake frosting - Pillsbury Vanilla or Milk Chocolate	1 Tub 16oz/1lb	CRC 2,185.00	$3.64	2 Tbsp 33g	CRC 158.96	$0.26
Cake Mix - Pillsbury French Vanilla or Chocolate	1 Box	CRC 1,770.00	$2.95	1 Slice 75g	CRC 147.50	$0.25
Tortilla Corn - Tortirica (20 count)	Pk	CRC 1,310.00	$2.18	1 Whole	CRC 65.50	$0.11
Tortilla Flour - Mission (12 count)	Pk	CRC 680.00	$1.13	1 Whole	CRC 56.67	$0.09

Meat

INGREDIENT	Amount	PRICE ¢ - Colones	PRICE $ -Dollars	SERVING/ AMT	SERVING PRICE ¢	SERVING PRICE $
Beef Ground 90%	Kilo	CRC 7,335.00	$12.23	3oz / 85g	CRC 623.83	$1.04
Beef Ground 95%	Kilo	CRC 8,025.00	$13.38	3oz / 85g	CRC 682.13	$1.14
Beef Steak Rib eye	Kilo	CRC 14,230.00	$23.72	3oz / 85g	CRC 1,209.55	$2.02
Beef Steak Sirloin Steer	kilo	CRC 13,005.00	$21.68	3oz / 85g	CRC 1,105.43	$1.84
Beef Steak Sirloin Porterhouse	kilo	CRC 17,405.00	$29.01	3oz / 85g	CRC 1,479.43	$2.47
Beef Steak Tenderloin	Kilo	CRC 18,030.00	$30.05	3oz / 85g	CRC 1,532.55	$2.55
Chicken Fillet (3.5oz)	Kilo	CRC 3,900.00	$6.50	1 Breast 3.5oz	CRC 390.00	$0.65
Chicken Legs	Kilo	CRC 4,295.00	$7.16	1 Leg	CRC 715.83	$1.19
Chicken Wings	Kilo	CRC 2,180.00	$3.63	1 Wing	CRC 136.25	$0.23
Fish Red Snapper Fillet	kilo	CRC 14,550.00	$24.25	3oz / 85g	CRC 1,236.75	$2.06
Fish Shrimp 600g 26/30	1 Bag	CRC 17,245.00	$28.74	4oz / 113g	CRC 1,955.55	$3.26
Fish Shrimp 600g 51/60	1 Bag	CRC 12,905.00	$21.51	4oz / 113g	CRC 1,463.40	$2.44
Fish Tuna Fillet	Kilo	CRC 14,070.00	$23.45	3oz / 85g	CRC 1,195.95	$1.99
Pork Chop	Kilo	CRC 3,785.00	$6.31	3oz / 85g	CRC 321.73	$0.54
Pork Loin Medallion	Kilo	CRC 10,335.00	$17.23	3oz / 85g	CRC 878.48	$1.46
Sliced Meats / Deli Meats (Turkey 255g)	Pk	CRC 2,995.00	$4.99	57g 9 slices	CRC 665.55	$1.11
Sliced Meats / Deli Meats Ham 255g)	Pk	CRC 2,995.00	$4.99	57g 10 slices	CRC 665.55	$1.11
Tuna In Oil (105g)	Pk	CRC 885.00	$1.48	55g	CRC 463.65	$0.77
Tuna In Water (105g)	Pk	CRC 1,600.00	$2.67	55g	CRC 838.20	$1.40

Beverages

INGREDIENT	Amount	PRICE ¢ Colones	PRICE $ Dollars	SERVING/ AMT	SERVING PRICE ¢	SERVING PRICE $
Coca Cola (Glass Bottle)	1 L	CRC 800.00	$1.33	12 ounce	CRC 283.90	$0.47
Coca Cola (Glass Bottle)	354 ml	CRC 600.00	$1.00	12 ounce	CRC 600.00	$1.00
Coca Cola (Returnable Bottle)	2.5 L	CRC 1,090.00	$1.82	12 ounce	CRC 154.73	$0.26
Coffee (9oz)	1 Bag	CRC 1,865.00	$3.11	2 Tbsp	CRC 213.36	$0.36
Coffee Powder Creamer (Senior Café - 13.05oz)	1 Bag	CRC 1,245.00	$2.08	1 tsp.	CRC 12.20	$0.02
Juice Box - Ve Bida D Frutas Mix (6-pack 1200ml)	Pk	CRC 1,115.00	$1.86	1 Box	CRC 185.83	$0.31
Orange Juice - Dos Piños	1.8L	CRC 1,600.00	$2.67	1 Cup	CRC 252.56	$0.42
Drink Mix - Sabe Mas (Mandarina Flavor)	Pk	CRC 125.00	$0.21	250 ml	CRC 27.78	$0.05
Drink Mix - Tang (Uva - Gape Flavor)	Pk	CRC 150.00	$0.25	240 ml	CRC 18.75	$0.03
Tea - Lipton (200 bags)	Pk	CRC 3,400.00	$5.67	1 Bag	CRC 17.00	$0.03

Alcohol

INGREDIENT	Amount	PRICE ¢ Colones	PRICE $ Dollars	SERVING/ AMT	SERVING PRICE ¢	SERVING PRICE $
Beer - Imperial (domestic 6-pack cans)	350ml	CRC 4,630.00	$7.72	1 Can 350ml	CRC 771.67	$1.29
Bacardi Rum Blanco	750ml	CRC 8,425.00	$14.04	1 Shot 42.6 ml	CRC 478.54	$0.80
Cacique Guaro	1000ml	CRC 4,975.00	$8.29	1 Shot 42.6 ml	CRC 211.94	$0.35
Flor De Caña Rum 4 year	1000ml	CRC 12,515.00	$20.86	1 Shot 42.6 ml	CRC 533.14	$0.89
Jack Daniels Whiskey	750ml	CRC 28,945.00	$48.24	1 Shot 42.6 ml	CRC 1,644.01	$2.74
Jose Cuervo Tequila	750ml	CRC 11,875.00	$19.79	1 Shot 42.6 ml	CRC 674.50	$1.12
Smirnoff Vodka	750ml	CRC 7,850.00	$13.08	1 Shot 42.6 ml	CRC 445.88	$0.74

Snacks

INGREDIENT	Amount	PRICE ¢ Colones	PRICE $ Dollars	SERVING/ AMT	SERVING PRICE ¢	SERVING PRICE $
Candy - Hershey's	43g	CRC 805.00	$1.34	1 Whole	CRC 805.00	$1.34
Candy - Skittles	43g61.5g	CRC 665.00	$1.11	1 Whole	CRC 665.00	$1.11
Candy - Snickers	1.86oz 52.7g	CRC 665.00	$1.11	1 Whole	CRC 665.00	$1.11
Chips - Corn Chirulitos 100g	1 Bag	CRC 680.00	$1.13		CRC 0.00	$0.00
Chips - Corn Doritos 7oz	1 Bag	CRC 2,475.00	$4.13	1oz 11 Chips	CRC 353.57	$0.59
Chips - Potato Del Volcan Papas 250g	1 Bag	CRC 2,655.00	$4.43		CRC 0.00	$0.00
Chips - Potato Lays Classic 200g	1 Bag	CRC 1,855.00	$3.09	1oz 15 Chips	CRC 65.43	$0.11
Chips - Pringles 124g	1 Can	CRC 1,410.00	$2.35	25g 13 Chips	CRC 282.00	$0.47
Chips - Corn Tortilla - Jacks Mejitos (300g)	1 Bag	CRC 1,200.00	$2.00	25g	CRC 100.00	$0.17
Chips - Corn Tortilla - Rumba (300g)	1 Bag	CRC 1,165.00	$1.94	25g	CRC 97.08	$0.16
Chips - Plantain Platanos Caribenos (28g)	Pk	CRC 580.00	$0.97	1 Whole	CRC 580.00	$0.97
Chips - Plantain Soldanza Platanos (180g)	Pk	CRC 955.00	$1.59	28g 30 chips	CRC 66.83	$0.11
Chips - Yucca (Yuquitas 350g)	1 Bag	CRC 1,990.00	$3.32	28g 25 chips	CRC 159.20	$0.27
Cookies - Cocanas (28 Count)	1 Bag	CRC 670.00	$1.12	4 Cookies	CRC 143.58	$0.24
Cookies -Oreo (12 Individual Packages- 4 Each)	Pk	CRC 1,800.00	$3.00	Pk	CRC 150.00	$0.25
Peanuts Planters (340g)	Can	CRC 3,110.00	$5.18	1oz	CRC 256.20	$0.43
Popcorn (400g)	Pk	CRC 515.00	$0.86	3 Cups Popped	CRC 36.50	$0.06

Preparation Information & Tips

Fruits

We have tested and it has been proven...simply cutting up fruit increases its consumption by 1 million percent. Okay, that might be a slight exaggeration, but the idea holds truth. We have had fruit literally rot on the counter because no one wanted to take the time to peal and cut it. On the other hand, if we do take the time to cut and peal it, the fruit disappears at an amazing pace. Let's face it, most people like convenience and can be lazy at times. It doesn't however take too much effort to grab a knife and cutting board and slice up some fruit to have on hand for a quick snack. Unfortunately, many people opt instead for a package of cookies or bag of chips.

The other thing to consider is that the peel is rarely very appetizing. When we reveal the juicy bright colored meat of the fruit, it gets our mouths watering. That isn't often the case with the outside of the pineapple or the rind of the melon. Consider a fruit salad. The vibrant colors and juicy sweetness make it hard to resist.

Make sure you keep this in mind when buying fruit. If you want it to be eaten, you should take the time to cut it up. Have a bowl on the counter for after school/work. Keep a container of cut fruit in the refrigerator for a quick grab during television, or gaming time. If you cut it they will eat it, and so will you.

Dairy

Holy cow! Dairy adds to your meal and it's not just the creamy flavor and gooey texture. Did you know that adding one slice of cheese, or one cup of shredded cheese to top off your tostada, adds approximately 100 calories and $0.60 per serving? That one tablespoon of sour cream may only add a few cents, but at 20 calories each, those spoonfuls can add up. It may not sound like much, but dairy products add about 30% to the price and calories. They also take up approximately 10% of your daily allowance of fat, and we're not talking the good fats either.

Processed cheese like cheese singles, cheese spray, and cheese dips are the least healthy. These products use a large amount of oil in processing, which adds unhealthy fats. If you must indulge your cheese cravings, try to stick with real cheese, or skim versions.

In addition to cheese, milk is a good source of calcium. Keep in mind that milk tastes different in Central America, as well. We prefer the taste of North American milk, but Costa Rican milk is still good for cereal and baking.

Nutrition wise, milk offers some great benefits, but at a cost. Calories are similar to that of cheese, at around 100 calories per cup, depending on the fat level. Milk is high in calcium and contains a good amount of protein. If you are looking to add calcium in your diet, milk is a better option than cheese. Other low calorie options of calcium include oatmeal and tomatoes.

Oils and Fats

Oils and fats are a staple for cooking. They not only provide additional flavor, but help keep foods from sticking together and to the pan. In certain cases, oils can also be used to transform things, like potatoes into French fries, or to create a crispy coating on chicken. Not to mention they are great for carnival food, like funnel cakes and deep-fried Twinkies. Frying food not only increases the flavor, but adds a considerable amount of calories and fat.

How you prepare your food is going to make a great impact on its nutritional value. A perfectly healthy meal can become extremely unhealthy, depending on the amount of oil ,or fat used to prepare it. This is the primary reason we often use our electric pressure cooker, as you don' t need to add oils and fats. Baking is another option to reduce fats and oils in your food.

When it comes to food preparation, there are a number of options when it comes to oils and fats. The fats you use can greatly impact both the health benefits and the cost of the meal. That's why it's important to understand the differences between various oils, including lard and animal fats.

There are many great resources on the Internet to find the pros and cons of different oils. One resource we found very helpful was a blog by Kimberly Alt at Earth Friends. Kimberly provides a chart that is easy to understand that shows the health benefits of the most common cooking oils. In addition, she discusses olive oil and why you shouldn't cook with it. Olive oil has a high flash point and when heated over 200 degrees, it releases free radicals and dangerous toxic fumes in the smoke. It is better to opt for an oil that can take high temperatures.

We use coconut oil in our recipes and prefer it over standard vegetable oil and olive oil. We enjoy the light flavor and the tropical feel it gives to our dishes. Coconut oil also contains good fats that your body needs to function optimally. Many locals use lard, as it is the cheapest fat option, but you get what you pay for when it comes to nutritional value. Coconut oil is a good balance for the cost and flavor.

While there are a variety of health benefits to cooking with and eating coconut oil, it can also be used topically. Coconut oil can be used to protect your skin from the damaging UV rays from the sun. It can also be used to relieve skin irritation and eczema, moisturize your skin, protect your hair from damage, and even as a natural deodorant. Aside from its benefits to our bodies, I have even used coconut oil to condition and restore the wood on my acoustic guitar. It truly has a multitude of uses.

Portion Size

One of the most impactful ways to change your health and stay in budget is to practice portion control. North America is home to the "Super Size" mentality. Many people are convinced that more is better and justify their decision by the added "value". Others often think they'll take any extra home and eat it later, but that rarely works. Food nearly always tastes best fresh, and many people don't have the self-control to stop eating.

Unfortunately, the long-term effect of this behavior is unhealthy. Many people have grown accustomed to larger meals, and it takes them considerably more to reach the feeling of being full. This means in essence you have to consume more to feel satisfied. More food means more calories and fat and more expense.

If you are curious about the volume of your food intake and calories, we encourage you to create a food journal. When we took the time to track what we were eating, we were shocked to discover the sheer volume that we consumed. Our calorie intake was two to three times the recommended daily amount. Our downfall was snacks and desserts, but beverages also had a big impact.

Once we understood what the proper portion sizes were, we began to scale back our meal sizes. As a result, we were able to re-train our bodies and brains to eat the proper amount. It now takes less food to achieve that "full" feeling. In addition, we only upsize our meal now if we are going to be splitting it with someone else. We also came to realize the true "value" is in healthy portions.

Nutrition Information Calculation

To help you better understand the impact these meals can have on your health, we have provided the nutrition information for you. We do not own or have access to a lab, so this information is based off research and calculation only. This information is meant to be a guide and not an absolute for nutrition value. We have no way to take into consideration the amount of nutrients lost in the cooking process, or are changed into compounds through the chemical process of adding heat.

Should you require specific and extremely accurate nutrition information, please consult your doctor, or a nutrition expert with access to the equipment to test your food

Recipes & Produce

We have provided information on many produce options here in Costa Rica. These fruits and vegetables can be found throughout much of Central America. Some produce options are available year round, while others are seasonal. This is in no way a complete list, but we have tried to provide some of the fruits and vegetables that you may not be used to. These produce options are local to the area, which generally keeps the cost down.

The recipes we've included are meals that we prepare on a regular basis. Most are prepared weekly while a few of the rich high-calorie recipes we reserve for special occasions. The majority of the meals are extremely affordable and offer great nutritional benefits, as well. Using these recipes as our primary meals, we have experience weight loss and better health. We have also been able to greatly reduce our grocery budget.

These recipes can also be found on our website:

https://cutthecrapcostarica.com/kitchen/kitchen-recipes/

Simply register and provide proof of purchase to access the complete list of recipes at any time. The web application also allows you to change the number of servings and updates the ingredients to reflect the amount needed. Once you are registered, you will be able to access the recipes wherever you have Internet access.

Fruits & Vegetables
Frutas y Vegetales

Apples

Fuji

Kilo: ₡4,095 ≈ $6.83

Serving: ₡745.29 ≈ $1.24

Gala

Kilo: ₡3,140 ≈ $5.23

Serving: ₡571.48 ≈ $0.95

Granny Smith

Kilo: ₡3,415 ≈ $5.69

Serving: ₡621.53 ≈ $1.04

Vegan   Gluten-free

Apples also referred to as Manzana in Spanish, can be found throughout Costa Rica. Depending on the time of year, you can find apples that have been grown in Costa Rica. However, most of the apples I seem to buy have been imported. They remind me of the apples I buy in Colorado. They are crispy and juicy and come in a variety of different colors from green, red, and yellows with hints of orange. You can find them in most of the stores, trucks along the sides of the road, and farmers markets.

Here is what Certified Health Coach Barbara Rodgers has to say about apples in her Bestselling book "Wholey Cow A Simple Guide To Eating And Living."

> *"The apple is considered to be one of the healthier foods available. Apples are rich in vitamin C and contain a fair amount of fiber. They have other healthful benefits and nutrients, like magnesium, vitamin B-6, iron, vitamin A and calcium. When you compare this to apple sauce, a processed version of an apple, you might find the content of vitamin C to be about the same or maybe higher, but the fiber content is lower. Other nutrients originally present in the apple might be missing.*
>
> *The apple sauce might contain added ingredients, such as high fructose corn syrup or another sweetener. This depends on the brand you are looking at, but have you ever wondered why the processed version has more ingredients?*
>
> *Obviously, a certain amount of ingredients are added to obtain a longer shelf life. Others may be added to make the product look a certain way. The bottom line is you should examine what you eat. The next time you are out grocery shopping, take a hard look at the food you are selecting. Perhaps you will make better choices if you open your eyes wider?"*

*Wholey Cow A Simple Guide To Eating And Living*Rodgers (25)*

Bestselling Author Barbare Rodgers

Nutrition Facts

Serving Size 1 Whole Fruit (182 Gram)

Servings 1

Calories 95

	% Daily Value *
Total Fat .3g	1%
Saturated Fat .1g	1%
Sodium 1.8mg	1%
Potassium 194.7mg	6%
Total Carbohydrate 25g	9%
Dietary Fiber 4.4g	18%
Sugars 19g	
Protein 5g	10%

Vitamin A 1%	Vitamin C 14%
Calcium 1%	Iron 1%
Vitamin B6 5%	Magnesium 2%

Percent Daily Values are based on a 2,000 calorie diet. Your daily value may be higher or lower depending on your calorie needs.

Bananas

Kilo: ₡1,200 ≈ $2.00

Serving: 1 small Banana: ₡50 ≈ $0.08

Vegan   Gluten-free

The bananas in Costa Rica are DELICIOUS! We prefer the small version, which are approximately four inches long. The standard eight-inch variety is great too. Both varieties of banana found in Costa Rica are sweeter than any we have eaten in the United States. The small version is especially sweet and is great for smoothies, snacks, and desserts.

In addition to the normal yellow bananas, Costa Rica offers green bananas. The green bananas, however, are not good to eat raw. They typically are very hard and the flavor is not very good either.

Green bananas are great for cooking and make a tasty treat. They work well for a side dish too. Green bananas can be prepared in the same manner as the plantain.

Along with convenience, taste, and great nutrition value; bananas are cheap, as well. They can be used as the main ingredient in a variety of recipes like desserts, smoothies, and pancakes and won't break your budget.

Health benefits of Bananas include:

1. *Maintains Blood Pressure* – Bananas are high potassium levels, so they help you maintain healthy blood pressure.

2. *Reduces Asthma Symptoms* – Bananas may help reduce the symptoms of asthma. That's because they are high in both fiber and potassium.

3. *Prevents Cancer* – Bananas are high in Vitamin C and fiber, which has been shown to help in cancer prevention.

4. *Promotes Heart Health* – Bananas are also good for your heart. Bananas contain a variety of nutrients that are beneficial to your heart including fiber, potassium, vitamin C and B6.

5. *Helps Manage Diabetes* – Since bananas are considered a low glycemic food and are high in fiber, they may be beneficial to those who have diabetes.

6. *Promotes Digestive Health and Stops Diarrhea* – Bananas are loaded with potassium and fiber and as a result, promote digestive health.

7. *Preserves Memory and Boosts Mood* – Bananas can also

boost your mood, since they contain the amino acid tryptophan.

*Megan Ware RDN LD

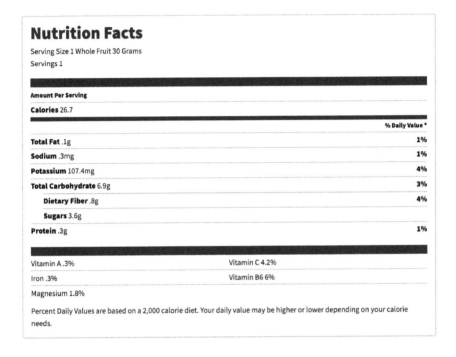

Nutrition Facts

Serving Size 1 Whole Fruit 30 Grams
Servings 1

Amount Per Serving

Calories 26.7

	% Daily Value *
Total Fat .1g	1%
Sodium .3mg	1%
Potassium 107.4mg	4%
Total Carbohydrate 6.9g	3%
Dietary Fiber .8g	4%
Sugars 3.6g	
Protein .3g	1%

Vitamin A .3%	Vitamin C 4.2%
Iron .3%	Vitamin B6 6%
Magnesium 1.8%	

Percent Daily Values are based on a 2,000 calorie diet. Your daily value may be higher or lower depending on your calorie needs.

Camote – Sweet Potatoes

Cost Per-Meal: ₡800 ≈ $1.33

Serving: ₡104 ≈ $0.17

Vegan   Gluten-free

Camote - sweet potatoes are a starchy vegetable, native to Costa Rica and Central America. Since they are readily available locally, they are extremely affordable food. As a result of being roots by nature, camote - sweet potatoes easily absorb nutrients in the earth. Some nutrients found in sweet potatoes include vitamin C, potassium, pantothenic acid (vitamin B5), niacin (vitamin B3), vitamin B6, manganese, magnesium, and copper. They are also high in fiber. Not only are camote - sweet potatoes high in vitamins, but they taste great too.

We enjoy making camote chips, mashed sweet potatoes, and adding them to soups. However, the easiest way to prepare camote as a side is to toss it in the electric pressure cooker. Once they are cooked, you can eat them as is or simply mash them.

Health benefits of Camote - sweet potatoes include:

1. *Strengthens Immune System* - Camote - Sweet Potatoes are high in vitamins A and C, so they help strengthen your immune system.

2. *Promotes Skin and Bone Health* - Camote - Sweet Potatoes are high in manganese, which helps build collagen and promotes both skin and bone health.

3. *Protects Against Aging and Disease* - Camote - Sweet Potatoes may help protect against the aging process and other diseases due to the antioxidants Vitamins A and C, which help protect cells.

4. *Helps Reduce the Risk of Obesity, Type 2 Diabetes, Heart Disease, and Cancer* – Camote - Sweet Potatoes contain high amounts of anti-inflammatory compounds, so they help reduce obesity, Type 2 diabetes, heart disease and cancer.

5. *Helps Control Sugar and Insulin Spikes*- Camote - Sweet Potatoes are high in fiber content, which makes them a slow-burning starch, so they can help control blood sugar.

6. *Helps Lower Blood Pressure*– Camote - Sweet Potatoes are high in potassium, which helps regulate heart rhythm.

7. *Helps Promote Weight Loss* – Camote - Sweet Potatoes contain resistant starch, which is a filling, fiber-like substance that helps promote weight loss.

*Cynthia Sass, MPH, RD

Nutrition Facts

Serving Size 1 Camote (130g)

Servings 1

Amount Per Serving

Calories 112

	% Daily Value *
Total Fat .1g	1%
Sodium 71.5mg	3%
Potassium 438.1mg	13%
Total Carbohydrate 26g	9%
Dietary Fiber 3.9g	16%
Sugars 5g	
Protein 2g	4%

Vitamin A 368%	Vitamin C 5%
Calcium 3%	Iron 4%
Vitamin B6 15%	Magnesium 8%

Percent Daily Values are based on a 2,000 calorie diet. Your daily value may be higher or lower depending on your calorie needs.

Chayote – Mirliton Squash

Kilo: ₡800 ≈ $1.33

Serving: ₡104 ≈ $0.17

Vegan   Gluten-free

Chayote - mirliton squash is a very common vegetable in typical Costa Rican cuisine. It can be found in many variations of casado, as a side in one form or another. You will often see it as a basic vegetable side, mixed in salads, or even made into a pickled relish. Chayote can be used in soups or other dishes to add nutrients and substance and is very versatile.

Chayote - mirliton squash, however, does not offer a

whole lot when it comes to flavor. It does not taste bad by any means, but rather has a very subtle flavor. Use chayote - mirliton squash to help dilute over-spiced dishes, or as a filler that will not overpower other ingredients.

Chayote - mirliton squash is a vegetable that boasts great health benefits. Since it doesn't contain cholesterol or unhealthy fats, it is often recommended for controlling cholesterol levels and weight loss. In addition, chayote is a great source of vitamin C, dietary fiber, potassium, magnesium, phosphorus, and choline.

Health benefits of Chayote - Mirliton Squash include:

1. *Digestive Health* - Chayote - Mirliton Squash may help with digestive health due to its high fiber content.

2. *Aids Weight Loss* - Chayote - Mirliton Squash is a high water content food that is low in fat. It is also low in calories. (38.6 calories, 0.1 grams of fat.)

3. *Helps Preserve Female Fertility* - Chayote - Mirliton Squash is abundant in folate, which helps prevent female fertility.

4. *Helps Prevent Cancer* - Chayote - Mirliton Squash is loaded with antioxidants that help fight free radicals.

5. *Maintain A Healthy Metabolism* - Chayote - Mirliton Squash also helps to maintain a healthy metabolism, since it contains the trace mineral potassium.

6. *Improve Immune System* - Chayote - Mirliton Squash may also help improve immune system function, since it contains the trace mineral zinc.

7. *Helps Develop Strong Bones*- Chayote - Mirliton Squash is rich in a variety of vitamins including: calcium, phosphorus, and magnesium, which help produce strong bones.
   *Robert Hughes

Nutrition Facts

Serving Size 1

Servings 1

Amount Per Serving

Calories 39

	% Daily Value *
Total Fat .3g	1%
Saturated Fat .1g	1%
Sodium 4.1mg	1%
Potassium 253.8mg	8%
Total Carbohydrate 9g	3%
Dietary Fiber 3.5g	15%
Sugars 3.4g	
Protein 1.7g	4%

Vitamin C 26%	Calcium 3%
Iron 3%	Vitamin E 1%
Vitamin K 10%	Thiamin 3%
Riboflavin 3%	Niacin 5%
Vitamin B6 8%	Folate 47%
Pantothenic Acid 5%	Phosphorus 4%
Magnesium 6%	Zinc 10%
Selenium 1%	Copper 12%
Manganese 19%	

Percent Daily Values are based on a 2,000 calorie diet. Your daily value may be higher or lower depending on your calorie needs.

Coconut Meat

Price Per Unit: ₡333 ≈ $0.56

Vegan   Gluten-free

People frequently get coconuts or pipas on the beach to drink the water, but then they throw the rest away. Unfortunately, they are missing some of the best parts of the coconut, the meat. Coconut meat is packed with a ton of nutrients and healthy fats.

This tropical delight is high in ascorbic acid, B vitamins, and proteins. In addition, it helps to restore oxidative tissue damage and is a source of healthy fats, proteins, and various vitamins and minerals. Coconut meat contains 17 amino acids out of the 20 amino acids needed for optimal protein formation–meaning it is great for building muscle mass. Do some research and soon you will see that the water is just the icing on the cake.

The easiest way to access the meat in coconut is with a machete or large knife. A few solid whacks and you'll soon be looking into the white bliss of tasty nutrition. Use a spoon to easily separate the meat from the shell. Then you can easily use a knife to cut the coconut into bite-size pieces.

We generally eat coconut meat raw. We have tried toasting it and baking it too, but we usually don't want to wait to cook it. It is great to eat it fresh right out of the shell.

Health benefits of Coconut Meat:

1. *Helps Maintain Good Cholesterol Levels-* Coconut Meat contains medium fatty acids, which unlike long chain fatty acids do not promote high cholesterol.

2. *Boosts the Immune System -* Coconut Meat is high in antioxidants and contains the trace mineral manganese, which help boost the immune system.

3. *Reduces Inflammation –* Since coconut meat has high levels of antioxidants, it helps reduce inflammation in the body.

4. *Healthy Digestion -* Coconut Meat is high fiber, so it promotes healthy digestion.

5. *Supports the Nervous Systems -* Coconut meat contains high amounts of the trace mineral manganese, which helps support the nervous system.

6. *Promotes Heart and Cell Health -* Coconut meat also helps promote heart health, as it contains the minerals potassium and copper.

*Lisa Thompson, CNH, HHP, CMT, PT

Nutrition Facts

Serving Size 1 Coconut (397 Grams)

Servings 1

Amount Per Serving

Calories 1405

	% Daily Value *
Total Fat 133g	205%
Saturated Fat 118g	590%
Sodium 79.4mg	4%
Potassium 1413.3mg	41%
Total Carbohydrate 60g	20%
Dietary Fiber 36g	144%
Sugars 25g	
Protein 13g	26%

Vitamin C 21%	Calcium 5%
Iron 53%	Vitamin B6 10%
Magnesium 31%	

Percent Daily Values are based on a 2,000 calorie diet. Your daily value may be higher or lower depending on your calorie needs.

Coconut Water

Price Per Unit: ₡333 ≈ $0.56

Vegan   Gluten-free

"Pipa, Pipa Fria", you can hear the calls of the peddlers on the beach, as they offer the natural refreshment of a cold coconut (pipa fria). But why only enjoy this tropical delight at the beach?

Honestly, coconuts are much cheaper to purchase at the ferias and you can take them to the beach with you in a cooler. Or you can simply throw them in your bag with a metal straw, and away you go. They are great for road trips and hikes as well. The refreshing treat is a great alternative to sodas and other sugary drinks.

In case you didn't catch it, metal straws are the key. Because they are metal, you can simply puncture the carpels (holes) and begin to enjoy without the need of a knife or machete to access the water. Otherwise, you will need to carry one of these tools with you in order to access the tasty goodness, which isn't a totally bad idea. With a machete or knife, you are able to access the meat of the fruit, as well.

One serving of coconut water equals 1 cup. A quick review of the nutrition content will show that you can consume multiple servings however, with few negative impacts on your health. Coconut water is high in potassium, but for most individuals, this is not a problem. Most Americans don't get enough potassium in their diet.

Health benefits of Coconut Water:

1. *Improves Cell Health and Reduces Risk of Disease* – Coconut water may promote cell health and help reduce the risk of illness, as it is loaded with antioxidants.

2. *Manages Diabetes and Regulates Blood Sugars* – Coconut water is also good for the management of blood sugar, since it is low on the glycemic index, high in fiber, and high in magnesium.

3. *May Prevents Kidney Stones* – Coconut water is very hydrating and may help reduce free radical production, which in turn may help prevent crystals from forming and sticking to the kidneys that can form stones.

4. *Supports Heart Health* – Coconut water has been shown to reduce cholesterol and triglyceride levels, which in turn help with heart health.

5. *Reduces Blood Pressure* – Coconut water is high in potassium, which helps reduce blood pressure.

6. *Restores Hydration* – Coconut water helps replenish the electrolytes potassium, magnesium, sodium, and calcium lost during exercise.

*Franziska Spritzler, RD, CDE

Nutrition Facts

Serving Size 1 Cup
Servings 1

Amount Per Serving

Calories 45

	% Daily Value *
Total Fat .5g	1%
Saturated Fat .4g	2%
Sodium 252mg	11%
Potassium 600mg	18%
Total Carbohydrate 9g	3%
Dietary Fiber 2.6g	11%
Sugars 6g	
Protein 1.7g	4%

Vitamin C 9%	Calcium 5%
Iron 3%	Vitamin B6 5%
Magnesium 15%	

Percent Daily Values are based on a 2,000 calorie diet. Your daily value may be higher or lower depending on your calorie needs.

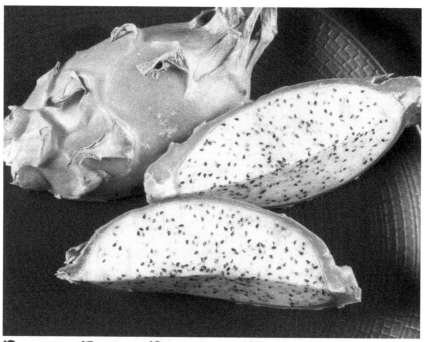

Dragon Fruit – Pitaya or Pitahaya

Kilo: ₡3500 ≈ $5.83

Serving: ₡693 ≈ $1.16

Vegan   Gluten-free

Dragon fruit also known as pitaya or pitahaya is the fruit of several different cactus species indigenous to the Americas. In Costa Rica, dragon fruit can be found in the dry stony areas of the Guanacaste and northern Puntarenas provinces, as these are the aridest parts of the country it is very common to find dragon fruit in the ferias and fruit stands from the months of

June to November when they are in season.

The spiny outsides of the ripe fruit will be either pink or yellow. If it is still green it is not yet ripe or ready to be picked. Cutting through the skin exposes the gelatinous pulp. The meat of this exotic fruit is vibrant purple or bleach white with speckles of black seeds. This colorful fruit leaves a serious stain, so be careful. Dragon fruit is often used in smoothies to produce an enticing bright colored drink.

Health benefits of Dragon Fruit include:

1. *High in Nutrients* – Dragon fruit is low in calories and packed with essential vitamins and minerals. It is also high in dietary fiber.

2. *May Help Fight Chronic Disease*- Dragon fruit is high in antioxidants and other nutrients your body needs to help fight off chronic disease including: vitamin C, Betalains, and Carotenoids.

3. *Helps Prevent Heart Disease, Type 2 Diabetes and More*- Dragon Fruit is high in fiber, which helps prevent a variety of illnesses and may help you maintain a healthy body weight.

4. *Promotes a Healthy Gut* – Dragon contains prebiotics, a specific type of fiber that helps promote the growth of healthy bacteria in your gut.

5. *Strengthens Your Immune System* – Dragon fruit contains Vitamin C and carotenoids that can help boost your immune system, as well as help prevent infection.

6. *May Boost Low Iron Levels* – Dragon Fruit is high in iron, so it can be beneficial for those suffering from iron deficiency or iron deficiency anemia.

7. *Converts Food Into Energy, Aids In Muscle Contraction, Forms Bones* – Dragon fruit contains high levels of magnesium, which helps convert food into energy and creates DNA. It also aids in muscle contraction and helps with the formation of bones.

*Makayla Meixner

Nutrition Facts

Serving Size 1 Fruit (198g)

Servings 1

Amount Per Serving

Calories 61	Calories from Fat 4.7

	% Daily Value *
Total Fat .5g	1%
Sodium 6.9mg	1%
Potassium 312mg	9%
Total Carbohydrate 15g	5%
Dietary Fiber 3g	12%
Sugars 9g	
Protein 1.1g	3%

Vitamin A 1.7%	Vitamin C 155%
Calcium 2.8%	Iron 1.7%

Percent Daily Values are based on a 2,000 calorie diet. Your daily value may be higher or lower depending on your calorie needs.

Granadilla & Maracuyá– Passion Fruit

Granadilla: 1 Fruit ₡200 ≈ $0.33

Maracuyá Kilo ₡1500 ≈ $2.50

1 Fruit: ₡375 ≈ $0.63

Vegan   Gluten-free

Granadilla & Maracuyá - Passion Fruit is a very common fruit you can find throughout Costa Rica. There are two varieties of passion fruit: the granadilla and the maracuyá. The difference between them is kind of like that of red and green apples; however, passion fruit tastes nothing like apples. The granadilla is usually the preferred version, as it is much sweeter and has a clear/translucent juicy pulp. The maracuyá is more sour, especially the reddish colored version with a yellowish pulp.

Nikki prefers the sour maracuyá with a sprinkle of salt, while the rest of us prefer the sweeter granadillas. Most people spit out the seeds as you do with watermelons, but Nikki eats the seeds, as they have many health benefits. Either version works great in a smoothie and don't worry about the seeds because you can blend them up with the rest of the pulp. While the seeds are safe to eat, the fruit's hard outer skin isn't usually considered edible.

Nutrition information for granadilla & maracuyá- passion fruit is based on the standard passion fruit. No specific information was available for the Costa Rica species.

Health benefits of Granadilla & Maracuyá - Passion Fruit:

1. *Helps Boost Immunity*- Granadilla & Maracuyá - Passion Fruit is high antioxidants and other nutrients that help boost immunity.

2. *Protects Cells* - Granadilla & Maracuyá - Passion Fruit protect cells through antioxidants.

3. *Promotes Eye Health*- Granadilla & Maracuyá - Passion Fruit is high Vitamin A, which helps promote eye health.

4. *Aids In Digestion* - Granadilla & Maracuyá - Passion Fruit aids in the digestion process due to its rich fiber content.

5. *Improves Heart Health*- Granadilla & Maracuyá - Passion Fruit contains high levels of potassium, which helps reduce blood pressure and may help improve heart health.

6. *Improves Circulation-* Granadilla & Maracuyá - Passion Fruit is high in potassium, iron, and copper, which may help improve circulation.

7. *Good For Bone health-*Since Granadilla & Maracuyá - Passion Fruit is rich in iron, magnesium, copper, and phosphorus, it is good for your bones.

8. *Helps Reduce Insomnia-* Granadilla & Maracuyá - Passion Fruit contains a medicinal alkaloid called Harman, which actually works as a sedative. It has been shown to help with sleep, anxiety, and restlessness.

*John Staughton (BASc, BFA)

Nutrition Facts

Serving Size 1 Whole Fruit (18 Grams)
Servings 1

Amount Per Serving

Calories 17

	% Daily Value *
Total Fat .1g	1%
Sodium 5mg	1%
Potassium 62.6mg	2%
Total Carbohydrate 4.2g	2%
Dietary Fiber 1.9g	8%
Sugars 2g	
Protein .4g	1%

Vitamin A 4%	Vitamin C 9%
Iron 1%	Magnesium 1%

Percent Daily Values are based on a 2,000 calorie diet. Your daily value may be higher or lower depending on your calorie needs.

Guanabana – Soursop

Kilo: ₡2,000 ≈ $3.33

Serving 1 cup: ₡450 ≈ $.075

Vegan   Gluten-free

Guanabana - Soursop is a very common fruit found in Costa Rica. These massive green fruit with spiny skin grow abundant in Costa Rica. They often splatter when they drop from the trees when they are not harvested. Once you cut through the skin of the guanabana - soursop, the beautiful white pulp and shiny black seeds are revealed. The meat is juicy, soft, and custard-like. While some people believe it tastes similar to mango mixed with pineapple, or strawberries and apples, our family thinks it just tastes like Hubba Bubba bubble gum. Many use guanabana to make ice cream or in smoothies.

Health benefits of Guanabana - Soursop include:

1. *Prevent Cell Damage & Lowers the Risk of Chronic Disease* - with high in antioxidants.

2. *May Help Kill Cancer Cells* – Some studies show that Guanabana – Soursop may help kill cancer cells due to its high antioxidants levels that help with free radicals.

3. *Helps Fight Bacteria* - Guanabana – Soursop has powerful antibacterial properties, as well as high antioxidant levels that may help kill cancer cells.

4. *Helps Reduce Inflammation* - Guanabana – Soursop is nutrient dense and chock-full of antioxidants that may help reduce inflammation.

5. *Helps Stabilize Blood Sugar Levels* – Studies show that Guanabana – Soursop may help stabilize blood sugar levels, which is good news if you are diabetic.

*Rachael Link, MS, RD

Nutrition Facts

Serving Size 1 Cup (225g)
Servings 1

Amount Per Serving

Calories 148

	% Daily Value *
Total Fat .7g	2%
Saturated Fat .1g	1%
Sodium 31.5mg	2%
Potassium 625.5mg	18%
Total Carbohydrate 38g	13%
Dietary Fiber 7g	29%
Sugars 30g	
Protein 2.3g	5%

Vitamin C 77%	Calcium 3%
Iron 7%	Vitamin B6 5%
Magnesium 11%	

Percent Daily Values are based on a 2,000 calorie diet. Your daily value may be higher or lower depending on your calorie needs.

Mamón Chino – Rambutan

Kilo: ₡1500 ≈ $2.50

Serving: ₡42 ≈ $0.07

Vegan   Gluten-free

Would you eat that weird looking fruit? We would! Mamón Chinos are DELICIOUS!

Mamón Chinos are also known as Rambutan. These red hairy treats are the perfect snack for a day at the beach, or to throw in your backpack for a hike in the jungle.

The name mamón chino is directly translated as "Chinese sucker," which is a great description for this fruit that originates from Asia. The outer skin is tough, while the hairs help protect it. You can use a knife, or just your fingernail to penetrate the skin. Then, peel it back to expose the almost translucent white meat of the fruit.

The meat of the fruit is a very firm, gummy type jelly that is similar to a grape, but much more congealed. The taste is a bit like a cross between a grape and a pear, but not exactly. The center holds a large pit, so don't just bite into it. Once you peel it, bite into the mamón chino meat and eat around the seed.

We love the crazy look of this delightful treat, but the taste is definitely the best part. They are also portable and pack easily in a bag for activities. They are affordable too, making them one of our favorite fruits.

Mamón Chino - Rambutan are plentiful during, their growing season, which is typically July through October. This may vary slightly depending on what region of Costa Rica you are in.

Rambutan fruit contains a variety of nutrients including vitamin C, potassium, iron, beta carotene or vitamin A, magnesium zinc, sodium, niacin, fiber, protein, and a little calcium.

Health benefits of Mamón Chino - Rambutan include:

1. *Disease Prevention (Cancer, Coronary Heart Disease, Diabetes)* - Mamón Chino - Rambutan contains high amounts of antioxidants, so it is useful in the prevention of a variety of illnesses including: cancer, coronary heart disease, and diabetes.

2. *Stabilizes Blood Sugar* - Mamón Chino - Rambutan has a high in fiber content, so it helps stabilize blood sugar.

3. *Promotes Digestive Health* - Mamón Chino – Rambutan is loaded with fiber, so aids in the digestive process.

4. *Supports Strong Bones* - Mamón Chino - Rambutan contains a variety of vitamins including manganese, which helps support strong bones.

5. *Helps Fight off Infections*- Mamón Chino – Rambutan contains a number of antimicrobial properties, which help fight off infections and optimize health.

*Rachael Link, MS, RD

Nutrition Facts

Serving Size 1 Whole Fruit 28g
Servings 1

Amount Per Serving

Calories 22.96

	% Daily Value *
Total Fat 5.9g	10%
Sodium 3.1mg	1%
Potassium 11.8mg	1%
Total Carbohydrate 5.8g	2%
Dietary Fiber .3g	2%
Protein .2g	1%

Vitamin C 1.7%	Calcium .6%
Iron .9%	Niacin 2.5%
Folate .6%	Phosphorus .3%
Magnesium .5%	Manganese 4.5%

Percent Daily Values are based on a 2,000 calorie diet. Your daily value may be higher or lower depending on your calorie needs.

Mango

Kilo: ₡1,400 ≈ $2.33

Serving: ₡900 ≈ $1.50

Vegan   Gluten-free

Mangoes are a great snack and a perfect addition to fruit salads, smoothies, and desserts. This tropical fruit is packed with nutrients and has a delicious flavor. The bright yellow meat brings vibrancy to any plate. Its sweet tropical taste always brings thoughts of warm sunshine and great days.

Mangoes are very common in Costa Rica and are available in a multi-color variety like green, yellow, orange, and red. Most mangoes found in ferias and supermercados are very large. Other varieties found throughout Costa Rica are slightly smaller and are yellow in color. They typically are sweeter and juicier and are our favorite.

One serving of mango contains the TOTAL recommended amount of Vitamin C, and that's just the beginning! Mangoes offer a multitude of health benefits including weight loss, and cancer prevention. They also aid in digestion, boosts immunity, promote eye health, lower cholesterol and help clear the skin.

Note: Nutrition facts are based on 336 grams. This is about half of a Costa Rica Mango. They are huge compared to the mangoes we used to buy in the states.

Health benefits of Mango include:

1. *Helps Prevent Cancer* – Mangos are loaded with antioxidants, which are useful in the prevention of cancer.

2. *Lowers Cholesterol* – Mangos may help lower cholesterol due to their high levels of pectin, vitamin C and fiber.

3. *Clears the Skin* –Mangos help clear the skin. They help clear both clogged pores and elim-inate pimples.

4. *Improves Eye Health* – Mangos are rich in Vitamin A, so are beneficial for eye health.

5. *Alkalizes the Whole Body* – Mangos contain tartaric acid, malic acid, and a trace of citric acid, which helps alkalize the body.

6. *Helps with Diabetes* – Mangos have a relatively low glycemic index, which helps stabilize blood sugar levels.

7. *Helps Fight Heat Stroke* - Drinking raw mango juice may help prevent heat stroke because it is high in sodium chloride.

8. *Boosts the Immune System* –Mangos contain Vitamin C and A, plus it over25 different carotenoids, which helps boost the immune system.
   *Diana Herrington

Nutrition Facts

Serving Size 1/2 Fruit
Servings 1

Amount Per Serving

Calories 201

	% Daily Value *
Total Fat 1.3g	2%
Saturated Fat .3g	2%
Sodium 3.4mg	1%
Potassium 564.5mg	17%
Total Carbohydrate 50g	17%
Dietary Fiber 5g	20%
Sugars 46g	
Protein 2.8g	6%

Vitamin A 72%	Vitamin C 203%
Calcium 3%	Iron 2%
Vitamin B6 20%	Magnesium 8%

Percent Daily Values are based on a 2,000 calorie diet. Your daily value may be higher or lower depending on your calorie needs.

Melon – Cantaloupe

Kilo: ₡895 ≈ $1.49

Serving 1 Cup: ₡152.15 ≈ $0.25

Vegan   Gluten-free

Cantaloupe melon is very common in Costa Rica and is often used in fruit salad and smoothies. Cantaloupe makes a very affordable breakfast, or snack at just $0.25 per cup. Cantaloupe is a great alternative to crackers or chips, which have more calories and fats.

Similar to watermelon, the cantaloupe has a tough exterior, which makes it a great beach snack too. Simply throw one in your bag, along with a knife. Cantaloupe is also great to take along to soccer games, a park, or pretty much any outdoor activity.

As a side, the bright orange color helps bring vibrancy to an otherwise bland plate. Because of its sweet taste, it complements a number of main courses, as well. And with the low cost, it adds a variety of nutrients and flair, while keeping the plate cost down.

Health benefits of Melon - Cantaloupe include:

1. *Protects Eyesight* - Melon – Cantaloupe contains a variety of vitamins, as well as the antioxidant zeaxanthin, which helps protect your eyes.

2. *Decreases Blood Pressure and Promotes Heart Health-* Melon – Cantaloupe contains fiber, potassium, vitamin C, and choline, which all help stabilize blood pressure and promote heart health.

3. *Protects Against Cancer* – Since Melon – Cantaloupe is rich in beta-carotene, it may help in the protection of cancer.

4. *Promotes Healthy Digestion-* Melon – Cantaloupes have a high fiber and water content, so they help promote healthy digestion.

5. *Helps you stay hydrated* - Melon – Cantaloupe have high water content and are loaded with electrolytes, so they help keep you hydrated.

6. *Helps Reduce Inflammation* – Eating Melon – Cantaloupe may also help reduce inflammation as they contain choline, which helps to maintain cellular structure, helps with the transmission of nerve impulses, and helps absorb fat.

* Megan Ware RDN LD

Nutrition Facts

Serving Size 1 Cup

Amount Per Serving

Calories 81

	% Daily Value *
Total Fat .2g	1%
Saturated Fat .1g	1%
Sodium 30.6mg	2%
Potassium 387.6mg	12%
Total Carbohydrate 15g	5%
Dietary Fiber 1.4g	6%
Sugars 14g	
Protein 9g	18%

Vitamin A 1%	Vitamin C 51%
Calcium 1%	Iron 1%
Vitamin B6 5%	Magnesium 4%

Percent Daily Values are based on a 2,000 calorie diet. Your daily value may be higher or lower depending on your calorie needs.

Papaya

Kilo: ₡840 ≈ $1.40

Serving 1 Cup: ₡157.92 ≈ $0.26

Vegan   Gluten-free

Papaya is one of the cheapest fruits you can find in Costa Rica. It can be eaten alone or used in fruit salads and smoothies. The yellow, green, and red skin of the papaya covers an extremely vibrant, orange meat, with a center full of black seeds. Use a large spoon to remove the seeds and then simply chop into chunks. You can eat it alone, or add it to a fruit salad. The papaya flavor is somewhat similar to a melon, but is not as sweet. The meat texture is also similar to a melon, but less firm.

Papaya is not only appealing to the eye, but has a ton of health benefits. Additionally, it can improve your overall health, when eaten on a regular basis.

Some health benefits of the papaya include:

1. *Lowers cholesterol*-Papayas are rich in vitamin C, fiber and antioxidants, which have been shown to hinder cholesterol build-up.

2. *May help aid weight loss* – Papayas are very low in calories, but high in fiber, so they aid in digestion.

3. *Boosts your immunity* – Papayas are nutrient dense and very high vitamin C, which helps boost your immune system.

4. *Great for your eyes* –Papayas are rich in vitamin A, so are beneficial for eyesight.

5. *Protects against arthritis* – Papayas are very high in vitamin C and are anti-inflammatory, so they are beneficial for suffering from arthritis.

6. *Improves digestion* –Papayas are rich in fiber, which aids in the digestions process.

7. *Helps ease menstrual pain* – Papayas contain an enzyme called papain, which helps regulate and ease menstrual periods.

8. *Prevents cancer* – Papayas are a rich source of antioxidants, phytonutrients, and flavonoids that help prevent free radical damage to cells.

9. *Helps reduce stress* – Papaya contains high levels of vitamin C, which studies show help regulate the flow of stress hormones.

*Sameer Jha - Health.India.com

Nutrition Facts

Serving Size 1 Cup (188g)

Servings 1

Amount Per Serving

Calories 81 | Calories from Fat 4.4

	% Daily Value *
Total Fat .5g	1%
Saturated Fat .1g	1%
Sodium 15mg	1%
Potassium 341mg	10%
Total Carbohydrate 20g	7%
Dietary Fiber 3.2g	13%
Sugars 15g	
Protein .9g	2%

Vitamin A 36%	Vitamin C 190%
Calcium 2.9%	Iron 2.6%

Percent Daily Values are based on a 2,000 calorie diet. Your daily value may be higher or lower depending on your calorie needs.

Pineapple

1 Fruit: ₡500 ≈ $0.83

Serving: ₡91.16 ≈ $0.15

Vegan   Gluten-free

Costa Rica has the sweetest and best-tasting pineapple that we have ever eaten! This amazing fruit is so juicy and delicious that it makes the perfect refreshing snack on a hot day. We make it a point to keep cut pineapple in our refrigerator, so we have it ready eat. Pineapple is definitely a staple in our diet here in Costa Rica.

Did you know, a single serving of pineapple contains 131% of the daily-recommended amount of Vitamin C?

Not only does pineapple help curb that sweet-tooth craving, but it is also extremely good for you. Make sure you check out the nutrition information to see all the nutrients your body receives, as you satisfy your sweet tooth.

Probably the most common and versatile way to eat pineapple is in chunks. Simply cut off the top and bottom. Remove the side, and cut around the core. The core is edible and has many nutrients, but it is hard, fibrous and does not hold much of the sweetness that you find in the outer meat.

Chopped pineapple is an extremely healthy and tasty snack. It is simple to pull out a bowl from the refrigerator to munch on. Pineapple chunks can also be added to a variety of dishes including pizza toppings, pineapple chicken, or pineapple pie.

Pineapple slicers are a must-have tool in the Costa Rican kitchen. Make sure you stock your kitchen with one. You can purchase pineapple slicers at some department stores and supermercados in Costa Rica, but they will carry a higher price than in the states. Quality and style selection are limited, as well. We have provided a link to our recommendation for your Costa Rica Kitchen here:

 https://cutthecrapcostarica.com/kitchen/recommended-products/

Slicing the pineapple creates rings that give an aesthetic appeal to many dishes. Not only is the bright yellow color pleasing to the eye, but the round shape is a great contrast to the standard block shape of chopping.

Although some people might think using the slicer wastes too much fruit on larger pineapples, you can use this waste to make juice. Both the outside portions of the pineapple with the skin and the core contain pineapple juice. This tasty nectar can be used to make drinks, top salads, or used to make sauces for cooking. Make sure you don't waste this nutrient-rich treasure.

Health benefits of Pineapple include:

1. *Boost Immunity* – Pineapples have a bunch of nutrients your body needs including high levels of Vitamin C, which help boost immunity.

2. *Treatment For Colds And Cough* – Pineapples contain bromelain, which helps reduce mucus and high levels of Vitamin C helps prevent colds.

3. *Helps Prevent Cancer* - Pineapples are loaded with anti-oxidants and contain various enzymes that prevent and shrink cancer cells.

4. *Reduces Inflammation* – Pineapples have high concentrations of bromelain, which helps reduce swelling and inflammation.

5. *Eye Health* – Pineapples are beneficial for eye health and help reduce the risk of macular degeneration because they contain antioxidant properties and high concentration of vitamin C.

*Barbara Rodgers, CHC

Nutrition Facts

Serving Size 1 Cup (chunks)
Servings 1

Calories 82

	% Daily Value *
Total Fat .2g	1%
Sodium 1.7mg	1%
Potassium 179.9mg	6%
Total Carbohydrate 22g	8%
Dietary Fiber 2.3g	10%
Sugars 16g	
Protein .9g	2%

Vitamin A 1%	Vitamin C 131%
Calcium 2%	Iron 2%
Vitamin B6 10%	Magnesium 4%

Percent Daily Values are based on a 2,000 calorie diet. Your daily value may be higher or lower depending on your calorie needs.

Plantain

Package of 7: ₡1000 ≈ $1.67

Serving: ₡142.86 ≈ $0.24

Vegan   Gluten-free

Plantains are extremely common throughout Central America making them an extremely affordable food. You will find plantains on nearly every casado (typical Costa Rican plates), which is no surprise because they are so prevalent in the area.

Plantains can be used for cooking at any stage of ripeness, but ripe ones can be eaten raw. Just like bananas, as the plantain ripens, it becomes sweeter and its color changes from green to yellow to black. Green plantains are firm and starchy, and they resemble potatoes in flavor. Foods like patacones or tostones are made by using the green. Locals use the ripe versions to make Fried Plantains.

Plantain nutrition information resembles the banana very closely. Since you get a large volume at a little price, plantains are a great "bang for the buck" so to speak. They can take a week or longer to ripen and since you can use them at nearly any stage they are a staple to have in your Costa Rica kitchen.

Health benefits of Plantains include:

1. *Digestive Health* – Plantains are good for digestive health because of their high fiber content.

2. *Weight Control* – Plantains may help reduce weight. That's because they are high in fiber and contain complex carbohydrates that help keep you full.

3. *Heart-Healthy* – Plantains are high potassium, which helps maintain the cells and fluid that control your blood pressure and keep your heart pumping.

* Jacquelyn Cafasso

Nutrition Facts

Serving Size 1 Medium (179g)

Servings 1

Amount Per Serving

Calories 218

	% Daily Value *
Total Fat .7g	2%
Saturated Fat .3g	2%
Sodium 7.2mg	1%
Potassium 893.2mg	26%
Total Carbohydrate 57g	19%
Dietary Fiber 4.1g	17%
Sugars 27g	
Protein 2.3g	5%

Vitamin A 40%	Vitamin C 54%
Iron 6%	Vitamin B6 25%
Magnesium 16%	

Percent Daily Values are based on a 2,000 calorie diet. Your daily value may be higher or lower depending on your calorie needs.

Watermelon – Sandia

Price:

Kilo: ₡500 ≈ $0.83

Serving: 1 Cup ₡76 ≈ $0.13

Vegan   Gluten Free

It is composed of approximately 92% water, and is a good source of Vitamin A, C, and B6. You can find it throughout Central America and can be bought in most stores year-round in Costa Rica. We love to buy watermelon - sandia from fruit stands and the back of local farmers' trucks and that are on the side of the roads on our way to local beaches.

Watermelon is a great fruit to throw in the car without getting smashed between all the beach gear. It is a quick and delicious snack to enjoy on the beach after an afternoon of surfing, or a long day of snorkeling. While we usually carry a pocketknife to cut the fruit, we've had to get creative a few times, by using shells and rocks to break open when we forgot our knife.

You will see more local farmers with full trucks alongside the road mid-February through May, which is typically harvest time. This is the cheapest time of year to buy this healthy fruit.

Health benefits of Watermelon - Sandia include:

1. *Helps You Stay Hydrated*- Watermelon Sandia contains 92% water, so it helps you stay hydrated.

2. *Assists in Preventing Cancer* - Watermelon Sandia may help prevent cancer by lowering the insulin-like growth factor (IGF) through the compound lycopene.

3. *Improves Heart Health* – Watermelon contains lycopene, citrulline (an amino acid), and Vitamins A, B6, C, magnesium, and potassium, all of which aid in heart health.

4. *Lowers Inflammation and Oxidative Stress* - Watermelon Sandia is anti-inflammatory and contains the antioxidants lycopene and vitamin C, which may help lower inflammation and oxidative stress.

5. *Prevents Macular Degeneration* - Watermelon Sandia contains lycopene, which helps prevent macular degeneration.

6. *Relieves Muscle Soreness* - Watermelon Sandia contains citrulline, an amino acid that helps relieve muscle soreness.

7. *Good for Skin and Hair* - Watermelon Sandia is good for both your skin and hair, as it contains high amounts of Vitamins A and C.

8. *Improves Digestion* - Watermelon Sandia aids in the digestion process due to its high water and fiber content.

*Kerri-Ann Jennings, MS, RD

Nutrition Facts

Serving Size 1 Cup

Amount Per Serving

Calories 46

	% Daily Value *
Total Fat .2g	1%
Sodium 1.5mg	1%
Potassium 170.2mg	5%
Total Carbohydrate 11g	4%
Dietary Fiber .6g	3%
Sugars 9g	
Protein .9g	2%

Vitamin A 17%	Vitamin C 20%
Calcium 1%	Iron 2%
Vitamin B6 5%	Magnesium 3%

Percent Daily Values are based on a 2,000 calorie diet. Your daily value may be higher or lower depending on your calorie needs.

Yuca – Cassava

Kilo: ₡600 ≈ $1.00

1 yuca 408g: ₡244.80 ≈ $0.41

Vegan   Gluten Free

Yuca, also known as cassava is a root that is very common throughout Central America. Traditional Costa Rican plates offer yuca as a fried side. In addition, yuca is used in soups and can be mashed. The supermercados (grocery stores) stock yuca chips that are crispy and delicious as well. Our favorite ways yuca is prepared is as fries and chips. They are a great snack while watching the game and compliment bar-b-que perfectly.

Yuca, also known as cassava is a root that is very common throughout Central America. Traditional Costa Rican plates offer yuca as a fried side. In addition, yuca is used in soups and can be mashed. The supermercados (grocery stores) stock yuca chips that are crispy and delicious as well. Yuca prepared as fries and chips are our favorite. They are a great snack while watching the game and compliment bar-b-que perfectly.

The yuca root produces several other products. Cassava flour is one great gluten, grain, and nut free option. Many celiacs and people with nut allergies use cassava flour to prepare their meals. You may not know this but, another product of yuca is tapioca. By drying the yuca into a powdery (or pearly) extract you create tapioca. That's right, the tapioca pudding comes from yuca. There are several ways to consume this amazing root.

Yuca - Cassava ranks third as the largest source of food carbohydrates in the tropics. People in these regions only eat more of the carbohydrates rice and maize (corn). Yuca has the ability to withstand difficult growing conditions, in fact, it's one of the most drought-tolerant crops. Because it is local to Costa Rica, yuca is a great ingredient to stay within budget while adding some great nutrients as well. We make sure to stock a couple of pieces in our kitchen.

Note: Processing yuca by peeling, chopping, and cooking it will significantly reduce its nutrition value. Powdered forms of yuca like tapioca have very limited nutritional value.

Health Benefits of Yuca - Cassava include:

1. *Boosts Immunity* – Yuca is nutrient dense and has a high Vitamin C concentration, so it may help boost immunity.

2. *Helps Protect The Skin* – Yuca may help protect the skin because it aids in the production of collagen and helps with skin elasticity. It also contains Vitamin C and anti-oxidants, which are also beneficial to the skin.

3. *Helps With Arthritis Symptoms* – Yuca contains anti-inflammatory properties, as well as manganese, which help ease arthritis symptoms.

*Barbara Rodgers, CHC

Nutrition Facts

Serving Size 408 Grams (1 whole)
Servings 1

Amount Per Serving

Calories 650

	% Daily Value *
Total Fat 1.1g	2%
Saturated Fat .3g	2%
Sodium 57.1mg	3%
Potassium 1105.7mg	32%
Total Carbohydrate 155g	52%
Dietary Fiber 7g	29%
Sugars 7g	
Protein 6g	12%

Vitamin A 1%	Vitamin C 140%
Calcium 6%	Iron 6%
Vitamin B6 20%	Magnesium 21%

Percent Daily Values are based on a 2,000 calorie diet. Your daily value may be higher or lower depending on your calorie needs.

Sides

el Entremés

Black Beans – Electric Pressure Cooker

Cost Per-Meal: ₡632.46 ≈ $1.05

Serving: ₡210.82 ≈ $0.35

Vegan Gluten Free

Black beans are a staple in the Costa Rican diet. You will find black beans as a side of some casados and breakfast plates. They can also be used in place of red beans for gallo pinto, a signature dish of Costa Rica. Black beans that have been refried and mashed are often found as a dip for patacones, also known as tostones.

Black beans are very versatile and can be used to make a variety of dishes. Soups, dips, sides, and even gluten-free brownies can be made from this bean. Black beans are packed full of vitamins and minerals. They also have medicinal properties for your body, which makes them a great staple in your diet.

Some health benefits associated with black beans include:

1. *Maintains Healthy Bones* - Black beans are high in iron. They also contain phosphorus, calcium, magnesium, manganese , copper and zinc, which help to maintain healthy bones.

2. *Lowers Blood Pressure* - Black beans are low sodium. They also contain potassium, calcium, and magnesium, which all help maintain and lower blood pressure.

3. *Wards Off Heart Disease* - Black beans are a good source of phytonutrients and potassium. They also contain folate, vitamin B6, and are cholesterol free; all of which help ward off heart disease.

4. *Prevents Cancer* - Black beans contain a number of nutrients that are useful in the prevention of cancer including: selenium, saponins, folate, and fiber.

5. *Manages Diabetes* - The high fiber content of black beans has been shown to help manage diabetes.

6. *Healthy Digestion* - Black beans are a high fiber food, so they help aid in digestion.

7. *Weight Loss* - Black beans are a good weight loss food, as they have a high fiber content.

*Ware, Megan, RD LD

Black Beans – Electric Pressure Cooker

YIELDS
3 Servings

PREP TIME
2 mins

COOK TIME
45 mins

TOTAL TIME
47 mins

Ingredients

- ☐ 1 cup Black Beans
- ☐ 4 Bay Leaves
- ☐ 1 Tbsp Cumin (or Chili Powder)
- ☐ ½ tsp Black Pepper
- ☐ ½ Tbsp Fresh Cilantro minced (7-10 sprigs)
- ☐ 1 Clove Garlic
- ☐ 3 cups Water

Preparation

1. Measure out the beans and rinse of debris, then add to the electric pressure cooker.

2. Mince the garlic and cilantro, and add to the pot.

Cook

3. Add the water and all remaining spices to the pot. Secure the lid and set to the "Beans" setting.

4. When the timer goes, off release the pressure. If you want softer beans, allow the black beans to sit under presser for an additional 5-8 minutes.

5. Once the pressure is released, drain any excess water.

6. Serve and enjoy.

Nutrition Facts

Serving Size 1 Cup
Servings 3

Amount Per Serving

Calories 86.9	Calories from Fat 2.8

	% Daily Value *
Total Fat .8g	2%
Saturated Fat .1g	1%
Sodium 4.4mg	1%
Potassium 252.4mg	8%
Total Carbohydrate 15.4g	6%
Dietary Fiber 5.5g	22%
Sugars .2g	
Protein 5.5g	11%

Vitamin A .8%	Vitamin C .6%
Calcium 3.2%	Iron 14.9%
Vitamin K .7%	Thiamin 4.3%
Riboflavin 2%	Niacin 1.3%
Vitamin B6 20.7%	Pantothenic Acid 2%
Phosphorus 5%	Magnesium 3.7%
Zinc 2.7%	Selenium 6.7%
Copper 5%	Manganese 28%

Percent Daily Values are based on a 2,000 calorie diet. Your daily value may be higher or lower depending on your calorie needs.

Chile Lime Chayote – Electric Pressure Cooker

Cost Per-Meal: ₡470.93 ≈ $0.78

Serving: ₡235.47 ≈ $0.39

Vegan   Gluten-free

If you are looking for an affordable side for any dish, give this Chile Lime Chayote a try. Prepared in an electric pressure cooker, it is easy to make and tastes great. Since chayote is a local vegetable it is a cheap way to fill your family's stomachs. The chili spice gives a zesty flavor to the nutrient-rich squash. This side is great with beef, fish, poultry, and pork, you can't go wrong with this simple side.

You can also substitute cumin for the chili powder. We prefer chili powder over cumin; however, chili powder can be hard to find in Costa Rica, especially in the smaller beach towns.

Note: Although the skin is edible, our family prefers to peal the chayote. Should you wish you can skip the pealing process, simply wash and remove the seed before cutting into desired sections.

Chile Lime Chayote – Electric Pressure Cooker

YIELDS
2 Servings

PREP TIME
5 mins

COOK TIME
23 mins

TOTAL TIME
28 mins

Ingredients

- [ ] 2 Chayote
- [ ] ½ Tbsp Cumin (or Chili Powder)
- [ ] 1 Tbsp Salt
- [ ] 1 tsp Rosemary
- [ ] ½ Lime (Limon Mandarina)

Preparation

1. Peel the chayote. Slice the chayote in half down the crease and remove the seed with a spoon. Cut chayote again to make 1/4 or 1/8 sections as desired.

2. Place the chayote pieces in a bowl. Cut the lime in half and squeeze one-half of the lime over the chayote pieces.

3. Mix all of the seasonings in a large bowl.

4. Toss the chayote in the seasoning bowl to cover it.

Cook

5. Place the chayote pieces in the electric pressure cooker.

6. Place the lid on the cooker and start it on the "Vegetable" or "Steam" setting, depending on your model.

7. When the timer goes off, release pressure, remove the lid and serve.

8. Serve with your favorite dipping sauce.

Nutrition Facts

Serving Size 1

Servings 2

Amount Per Serving

Calories 51.5

	% Daily Value *
Total Fat .8g	2%
Saturated Fat .2g	1%
Sodium 3495.5mg	146%
Potassium 298.5mg	9%
Total Carbohydrate 11.8g	4%
Dietary Fiber 4.4g	18%
Sugars 3.7g	
Protein 2.2g	5%

Vitamin A .8%	Vitamin C 34.5%
Calcium 5.8%	Iron 10%
Vitamin B6 10%	Magnesium 7.5%

Percent Daily Values are based on a 2,000 calorie diet. Your daily value may be higher or lower depending on your calorie needs.

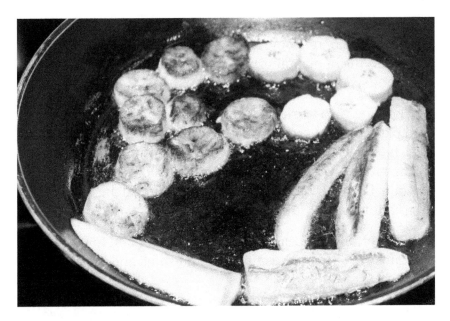

Fried Plantains

Cost Per-Meal: ₡398.96 $0.66

Serving: ₡199.48 $0.33

Vegan   Gluten-free

Fried Plantains are a delicious and very affordable treat. They can be eaten as snacks, sides, and even desserts. A staple to the Costa Rican diet; this delicious fare can be found on most casados (typical Costa Rican plates). Fried Plantains make a great side and add color and sweetness to an otherwise bland plate.

Since plantains take little preparation, they make a great snack. Instead of reaching for candy and baked goods, why not grab a serving of plantains instead? They are nutritious and can curb your sweet tooth.

Plantains also work great for dessert. Topping desserts with fried plantains is a great way to take your dessert to the next level. It is as easy as topping off your bowl of plain, vanilla ice cream with a few pieces of warm, bright colored, sweet fried plantain. Use your imagination to create some delicious, colorful creations of your own.

We typically use a small amount of coconut oil to fry our plantains. This keeps the nutrition value high and the fat and calories low.

Tip: We included the option to add sugar; however, we recommend trying them without sugar the first time. We do not usually add sugar when we prepare them for ourselves, but will sometimes add sugar for our guests, especially those from the U.S., who are accustomed to sugar being added to everything.

Fried Plantains

YIELDS
2 Servings

PREP TIME
3 mins

COOK TIME
20 mins

TOTAL TIME
23 mins

Ingredients

- [ ] 2 Ripe (black) plantains

- [ ] 1 Tbsp Coconut Oil (enough to coat the bottom of the pan)

- [ ] 1 tsp Sugar (optional to increase sweetness)

Preparation

1. Add coconut oil to coat the bottom of the pan. Heat pan on medium-high (approximately setting 5).

2. Peel and slice the plantain into desired shapes and sizes. We enjoy the bite-size round version, but long strips work better for certain desserts.

Cook

3. Place the plantain pieces in the pan and fry approximately 4-8 minutes, or until the bottoms are bright yellow or slightly brown.

4. Flip the pieces and fry another 3-6 minutes. If you prefer your plantains darker and crispier, flip again and fry for an addition 1-2 minutes.

5. *OPTIONAL - Top with sugar and allow to caramelize

6. Remove from the pan. Place the pieces on a plate, and let cool 3-5 minutes.

7. Eat and enjoy!

Nutrition Facts

Serving Size 1
Servings 2

Calories 399.5

Calories from Fat 181.5

% Daily Value *

Total Fat 20.2g	**32%**
Saturated Fat 16.8g	**85%**
Cholesterol 0mg	
Sodium 7.2mg	**1%**
Potassium 893.2mg	**26%**
Total Carbohydrate 57g	**19%**
Dietary Fiber 4.1g	**17%**
Sugars 27g	
Protein 2.3g	**5%**

Vitamin A 40%	Vitamin C 54%
Iron 6%	Vitamin B6 25%
Magnesium 16%	

Percent Daily Values are based on a 2,000 calorie diet. Your daily value may be higher or lower depending on your calorie needs.

Patacones

Cost Per-Meal: ₡ 2,097.71 ≈ $3.50

Serving: ₡1,048.86 ≈ $1.75

Vegan   Gluten-free

Patacones are typical Latin American food. In Costa Rica, they are found on many casados and offered as appetizers at several restaurants. Patacones are a delicious snack and can be used as an ingredient for a number of other meal options.

You can eat them alone like chips, or they can be topped with meat such as shredded beef, pork, or chicken. There are many ways to serve this fried banana/plantain treat. Use your imagination and create your own culinary masterpiece with patacones.

Green patacones make more potato like chips, whereas the yellow patacones are a bit sweeter. The green version holds together better and makes a better base to dishes where you top them.

If desired, you can add salt to increase the flavor. It will, however, change the nutrition value. When adding salt, we recommend sprinkling the salt on them immediately after removing them from the hot oil. This will allow the salt to stick better. We choose to forgo the salt, as we try to limit our sodium intake and appreciate the natural taste of the patacones.

Patacones

YIELDS	PREP TIME	COOK TIME	TOTAL TIME
2 Servings	5 mins	20 mins	25 mins

Ingredients

- ☐ 2 cups Coconut Oil
- ☐ 2 Plantains (green or yellow)

Preparation

1. Heat coconut oil in the pan on medium-high heat, (approximately 6.5 setting).

2. Cut the plantains into one-inch pieces.

Cook

3. Once the oil is hot, place the plantain pieces in the pan for two minutes.

4. Flip the plantain pieces, and cook for an additional two minutes, until yellow in color.

5. Remove from pan and smash the pieces with the bottom of a glass, or bowl to form chip shapes.

Tip: Use glasses or bowls without a lip on the bottom. The flatter and smoother the bottom is the better. If the plantains are sticking to the bottom of the glass or bowl, try coating the bottom with coconut oil, and use a knife to slide them off.

6. Place the plantain chips back in the oil to cook for an additional three minutes.

7. Flip the chips and cook two-three more minutes, until golden brown.

8. Remove the patacones from the oil, and place on a paper towel covered plate to cool. Once cool, plate your patacones and enjoy.

9. Once the oil has cooled, store the oil (approximately one cup) for the next time you fry food. (Nutrition information is based on 1 cup of Coconut oil).

Nutrition Facts

Serving Size 1
Servings 2

Amount Per Serving

Calories 3122 | Calories from Fat 2904

	% Daily Value *
Total Fat 312.7g	482%
Saturated Fat 264.3g	1322%
Sodium 7.2mg	1%
Potassium 893.2mg	26%
Total Carbohydrate 57g	19%
Dietary Fiber 4.1g	17%
Sugars 27g	
Protein 2.3g	5%

Vitamin A 40%	Vitamin C 54%
Iron 6%	Vitamin B6 25%
Magnesium 16%	

Percent Daily Values are based on a 2,000 calorie diet. Your daily value may be higher or lower depending on your calorie needs.

Popcorn – Stovetop

Cost Per 400 gram bag: ₡515 ≈ $0.86

Serving 3 Cups: ₡50.66 ≈ $0.08

Vegan   Gluten-free

Popcorn is a snack the whole family loves. It can be a healthy option too, depending on how you prepare it. We try not to add much salt to our popcorn to keep the sodium down. In addition, we use just enough oil to coat the bottom of the pan to prevent burning and sticking. Try using seasonings on your popcorn to add flavor instead of the traditional butter option. Seasonings can be another way to cut down on calories and fat.

We do not have an air popper for making popcorn, so we use the stovetop method, as it is cheaper and healthier than microwave versions. Besides, we think the stovetop popcorn just tastes better. Next time you are craving a crunchy snack, why not give popcorn a try instead of chips or crackers?

Popcorn – Stovetop

YIELDS
2 Servings

COOK TIME
10 mins

TOTAL TIME
10 mins

Ingredients

- ☐ 2 Tbsp Coconut Oil (enough to coat the bottom of pan)
- ☐ ¼ cup Popcorn

Cook

1. Coat bottom of the pan with coconut oil and heat on medium (approximately 6 setting).

2. Add popcorn to a saucepan with a lid and allow to cook.

3. When the popcorn starts to pop, use potholders to hold the lid on and gently shake the pan back and forth over heat, until there are roughly three seconds between pops.

4. Remove from heat and serve.

Nutrition Facts

Serving Size 3 Cooked Cups
Servings 2

Amount Per Serving

Calories 423   Calories from Fat 363

	% Daily Value *
Total Fat 42.3g	66%
Saturated Fat 33.6g	169%
Sodium .3mg	1%
Potassium 27mg	1%
Total Carbohydrate 6.9g	3%
Dietary Fiber 1.2g	5%
Protein 1.1g	3%

Iron 1.5%   Magnesium 3%

Percent Daily Values are based on a 2,000 calorie diet. Your daily value may be higher or lower depending on your calorie needs.

Red Beans- Electric Pressure Cooker

Cost Per-Meal: ₡603.46 ≈ $1.01

Serving: ₡201.15 ≈ $0.34

Vegan   Gluten-free

Red beans are a staple in the Costa Rican diet. You will find red beans as a side of some casados and breakfast plates, as an alternative to black beans. Red beans can also be used in gallo pinto, a signature dish of Costa Rica.

There are several health benefits associated with red beans, which are attributed to a variety of vitamins and minerals.

Health benefits of Red Beans include:

1. *Maintains Healthy Bones* - Red beans are great for helping to maintain healthy bones, since they are high in iron, phosphorus, calcium, magnesium, manganese, copper and zinc.

2. *Lowers Blood Pressure* - Red beans are a low sodium food. They also contain potassium, calcium, and magnesium, which all help lower blood pressure.

3. *Wards Off Heart Disease* - Heart disease is on the rise, which is why it is important to include more foods such as red beans in your diet. Red beans are high in phytonutrients and nutrients such as potassium, folate, vitamin B6 that help prevent heart disease. They are also cholesterol free.

4. *Prevents Cancer* - Red beans are high in selenium, saponins, folate, and fiber, so may help prevent cancer.

5. *Manages Diabetes* - Red beans have been shown to help manage diabetes, as they have a high-fiber content.

6. *Healthy Digestion* - Red beans aid in digestion, as they are high in fiber.

7. *Weight Loss* - Red beans aid in digestion, as they are high in fiber.

*Medical News Today

Red Beans- Electric Pressure Cooker

YIELDS
3 Servings

PREP TIME
2 mins

COOK TIME
45 mins

TOTAL TIME
47 mins

Ingredients

- ☐ 1 Tbsp Cumin (or Chili Powder)
- ☐ ½ tsp Black Pepper
- ☐ 4 Bay Leaves
- ☐ ½ Tbsp Fresh Cilantro minced (7-10 sprigs)
- ☐ Clove Garlic
- ☐ 3 cups Water

Preparation

1. Rinse the red beans of debris.
2. Mince the garlic and cilantro.

Cook

3. Place the beans, spices, and water in an electric pressure cooker and set to the "Beans" setting.
4. When the timer goes off, release the pressure. If you want softer beans, allow the beans to set under presser for an additional 5-8 minutes.
5. Drain excess water and serve.

Nutrition Facts

Serving Size 1 Cup
Servings 3

Amount Per Serving

Calories 86.3 | Calories from Fat 2.7

	% Daily Value *
Total Fat .8g	2%
Saturated Fat .1g	1%
Sodium 4.4mg	1%
Potassium 287.7mg	9%
Total Carbohydrate 15.1g	6%
Dietary Fiber 4.1g	17%
Sugars .2g	
Protein 5.5g	11%

Vitamin A .8%	Vitamin C 1.8%
Calcium 3.6%	Iron 15.6%
Vitamin K .7%	Thiamin 4.3%
Riboflavin 2%	Niacin 1.3%
Vitamin B6 20.7%	Pantothenic Acid 2%
Phosphorus 5%	Magnesium 3.7%
Zinc 2.7%	Selenium 6.7%
Copper 5%	Manganese 28%

Percent Daily Values are based on a 2,000 calorie diet. Your daily value may be higher or lower depending on your calorie needs.

Red & Black Beans – Electric Pressure Cooker

Cost Per-Meal: ₡617.96 ≈ $1.03

Serving: ₡205.99 ≈ $0.34

Vegan   Gluten Free

Red & Black Beans - Electric Pressure Cooker is basically a simple combination of the red bean and black bean recipes. We use this recipe often, as we like the color combination. When using red & black beans on tostadas or in beans and rice the two colors help give the dish a better presentation and appealing to the eye. Oh, and they taste great too!

Using the electric pressure cooker reduces the cook time and saves on energy while creating perfect been firmness. Red & Black Beans - Electric Pressure Cooker is another extremely affordable recipe that takes minimal time to cook. In addition, it makes a large amount, which is great! It is always nice to have some ready for another meal or two.

Red & Black Beans – Electric Pressure Cooker

YIELDS
3 Servings

PREP TIME
2 mins

COOK TIME
45 mins

TOTAL TIME
47 mins

Ingredients

- ☐ ½ cup Red Beans
- ☐ ½ cup Black Beans
- ☐ 2 Cloves Garlic
- ☐ 1 Tbsp Chili Powder (You can also substitute Cumin)
- ☐ ½ Tbsp Fresh Cilantro minced (7-10 sprigs)
- ☐ 2 Bay Leaves
- ☐ ½ tsp Pepper
- ☐ 4 cups Water

Preparation

1. Measure out the beans and rinse of debris, then add to the pot.

2. Mince the garlic and cilantro, then add to the pot.

3. Add the water and all the remaining spices to the pot.

Cook

4. Secure the lid and set to the "Beans" setting.

5. When the timer goes off release the pressure. If you want softer beans, allow the beans to set under presser for an additional 5-8 minutes.

6. Once the pressure is released, drain any excess water.

7. Serve and enjoy.

Nutrition Facts

Serving Size 1 Cup
Servings 3

Amount Per Serving

Calories 88.1 | Calories from Fat 2.8

	% Daily Value *
Total Fat .8g	2%
Saturated Fat .1g	1%
Sodium 4.6mg	1%
Potassium 274.1mg	8%
Total Carbohydrate 15.6g	6%
Dietary Fiber 4.8g	20%
Sugars .2g	
Protein 5.5g	11%

Vitamin A .8%	Vitamin C 1.7%
Calcium 3.5%	Iron 15.4%
Vitamin K 1.3%	Thiamin 8.7%
Riboflavin 4%	Niacin 2.7%
Vitamin B6 41.3%	Pantothenic Acid 4%
Phosphorus 10%	Magnesium 5.7%
Zinc 5.3%	Selenium 13.3%
Copper 10%	Manganese 56%

Percent Daily Values are based on a 2,000 calorie diet. Your daily value may be higher or lower depending on your calorie needs.

Rice – Electric Pressure Cooker

(Based off 99% white rice)

Kilo: ₡840, $0.52

Cost Per-Meal: ₡336, $0.56

Serving - ₡33.66, $0.06

Vegan   Gluten-free

Rice is very simple and is one of the most frequent things we cook. It is no wonder it is a staple in Costa Rica and is included in one form or another in every casado (typical Costa Rican plate). Rice is used to make Arroz con Pollo and Gallo Pinto, as well as in soups. Although you can make these dishes with fresh rice, it is common to make large batches and add the leftover rice to meals over the next few days. Gallo Pinto is almost always made with rice that was cooked a day or two prior.

Using the electric pressure cooker reduces cook time and saves energy, while creating perfect sticky rice firmness. Rice - Electric Pressure Cooker is another extremely affordable recipe that takes minimal time to cook. In addition, it makes a large amount for use in other meals. This recipe will produce approximately ten servings of plain rice

Rice – Electric Pressure Cooker.

YIELDS
5 Servings

PREP TIME
2 mins

COOK TIME
25 mins

TOTAL TIME
27 mins

Ingredients

- ☐ 2 cups Rice
- ☐ 4 cups Water

Prep

1. Measure 2 cups of rice. Rinse the rice to remove the debris and then add to the pressure cooker.

2. Add 4 cups of water to the pressure cooker.

Cook

3. Secure the lid to the pressure cooker and start on the "Rice" setting.

Note: If you prefer firm rice shorten the cook time by approximately four minutes.

4. When the timer goes off release the pressure.

5. Once the pressure is released remove lid and serve.

Seasoned Chili Yuca Fries

Cost Per-Meal: ₡678.15 ≈ $1.13

Serving: ₡339.08 ≈ $0.57

Vegan　　　　Gluten-free

Making French fries in Costa Rica is challenging because most potatoes are small. Yuca is a great alternative to the potato. They are a common vegetable throughout Central America making them extremely affordable in Costa Rica. The yuca fries have a slightly different texture and taste than the standard potato variety and we prefer them with many dishes. Seasoned Chili Yuca Fries make a great snack or the perfect bar-b-que side.

The Seasoned Chili Yuca Fries bring a little spice to the standard fry. Since they are baked they use a fraction of the oil making them a healthier option than the traditional deep-fried version. A great side for grill night or a snack while watching the game. Your family is sure to love these savory treats

Tip: We prefer our Seasoned Chili Yuca Fries to be very crispy so we leave them in the oven a bit longer. If you prefer softer fries add these additional steps:

1. PRIOR TO SEASONING, boil the cut yuca pieces in a pot of water for 10 minutes.

2. Adjust cook time to 15 minutes on each side..

Seasoned Chili Yuca Fries

YIELDS	PREP TIME	COOK TIME	TOTAL TIME
2 Servings	10 mins	37 mins	47 mins

Ingredients

- ☐ 2 Large Yuca
- ☐ 1 Tbsp Coconut Oil
- ☐ 1 tsp Salt
- ☐ ¼ tsp Black Pepper
- ☐ 1 tsp Chili Powder (if desired you can substitute cumin)

Preparation

1. Preheat oven to 400º Fahrenheit.

2. Peel the yuca to remove the waxy skin.

3. Chop the yucas in half and then slice into fry-shaped pieces of desired thickness.

   Note: Depending on your preferred fry thickness, you may need to adjust the cooking time.

4. In a large bowl combine the chili powder, salt, and pepper.

5. Add the coconut oil and yuca to the bowl and lightly toss until all pieces are coated.

6. Line the yuca pieces on a baking sheet allowing space between each piece.

Cook

7. Place the baking sheet in the oven and bake seasoned yuca fries for 15 minutes.

8. Remove yuca fries from the oven and flip with tongs or a fork.

9. Place the yuca fries back in the oven for an additional 15 minutes.

   Tip: Check the fries every few minutes to ensure the desired crispiness.

10. Plate and serve with your favorite dipping sauce.

Nutrition Facts

Serving Size 1

Servings 2

Calories 840.3   Calories from Fat 181.5

	% Daily Value *
Total Fat 21.1g	33%
Saturated Fat 16.8g	85%
Sodium 1223.3mg	51%
Potassium 1149.4mg	33%
Total Carbohydrate 156.3g	53%
Dietary Fiber 7.3g	30%
Sugars 7g	
Protein 6.4g	13%

Vitamin A 1.3%	Vitamin C 140%
Calcium 7.9%	Iron 13.6%
Vitamin B6 20%	Magnesium 22.7%

Percent Daily Values are based on a 2,000 calorie diet. Your daily value may be higher or lower depending on your calorie needs.

Slaw Salad

Cost Per-Meal: ₡573 ≈ $0.96

Serving: ₡286.50 ≈ $0.48

Vegan   Gluten-free

Slaw salad is another common food in Costa Rica. This nutrient-packed dish can either be the main course or a side to add color and crunch to your casado or other dinner plates. Aside from very few specific allergies, Slaw Salad is safe for almost all diets including Vegan and Gluten-free.

Tip: We enjoy adding a dash or two of hot sauce to add a bit of spice. We especially enjoy the Mango Hot Sauce from Jalapeños restaurant in Playa Negra, Costa Rica..

Slaw Salad

YIELDS
2 Servings

PREP TIME
10 mins

Ingredients

- [ ] 5 ½ cups Green Cabbage
- [ ] ½ cup Red/Purple Cabbage
- [ ] ⅛ Carrot
- [ ] ½ Large Radish
- [ ] ½ Sweet Pepper
- [ ] 1 Small Tomato
- [ ] 1 Small Onion
- [ ] ¼ Cucumber

Preparation

1. Slice equal portions of cabbage, carrots, radish, and peppers in two separate bowls. You can use a banjo/mandolin slicer.

2. Chop the tomatoes, cucumber and onions and add equal portions to each bowl.

3. Top with your favorite dressing.

Note: No dressing is included in the nutrition information.

Nutrition Facts

Serving Size 1

Servings 2

Calories 59.1	Calories from Fat 6.4

	% Daily Value *
Total Fat .8g	2%
Saturated Fat .2g	1%
Trans Fat 87.6g	
Cholesterol 411.9mg	138%
Total Carbohydrate 13.2g	5%
Dietary Fiber 4.9g	20%
Sugars 7.3g	
Protein 3.1g	7%

Vitamin A 75.3%	Vitamin C 106.4%
Calcium 20.9%	Iron 4.1%
Vitamin D 1.3%	Vitamin E .8%
Vitamin K 4.1%	Thiamin 1%
Riboflavin .6%	Niacin 1.2%
Vitamin B6 12.2%	Folate 4.9%
Pantothenic Acid .5%	Phosphorus 8.5%
Magnesium 8.7%	Zinc .1%

Percent Daily Values are based on a 2,000 calorie diet. Your daily value may be higher or lower depending on your calorie needs.

Breakfast

el Desayuno

Banana Pancakes – Gluten-Free

Cost Per-Meal: 795.70 ≈ $1.33

Serving: ₡397.85 ≈ $0.66

Gluten-free

You have to try these banana pancakes! They not only are nutritious, but they taste great too! This is a great gluten-free option to the standard pancake that everyone will enjoy. These Banana Pancakes are low in calories and are nutrient rich.

Note: The banana pancakes will remain moist even when fully cooked. If you are unsure if they are fully cooked, we recommend cooking for longer times on lower heat to ensure the middle is cooked through. In addition, you may need to flip the banana pancakes multiple times to avoid burning the outside.

Tip: For non-gluten-free banana pancakes, simply use regular flour in place of the gluten-free flour. We feel the flavor and way it cooks is worth the price difference.

Banana Pancakes – Gluten-Free

YIELDS 2 Servings   **PREP TIME** 4 mins   **COOK TIME** 11 mins   **TOTAL TIME** 15 mins

Ingredients

- [ ] 8 Small Bananas (2 medium)

- [ ] 1 Tbsp Coconut Oil

- [ ] 4 Eggs

- [ ] 2 Tbsp Gluten Free Flour (We prefer Jinca Foods brand Panadería Y Repostería gluten-free flower

Preparation

1. Coat the bottom of a frying pan with coconut oil and heat on medium heat (approximately setting 5.5).

2. Peel the bananas and smash them with a fork on a plate.

3. In a mixing bowl, beat the eggs with a mixer on medium speed for 30 seconds.

4. Add the flour and mix with the eggs for 15 seconds.

5. Add the bananas and mix for an additional 15 seconds.

Cook

6. Using a 1/4 measuring cup, scoop the batter into the pan for uniform size pancakes.

7. Cook the pancakes until you see bubbles forming on the surface. The bottoms should be golden brown (approximately 1 minute).

8. Once the sides begin to pull away from the pan, flip and cook an additional minute, until both sides are golden brown.

Note: You may need to adjust your stove temperature if the pancakes are burning on the bottom without cooking the middle.

9. Once both sides are golden brown, plate the pancakes with desired topping and sides.

Nutrition Facts

Serving Size 3
Servings 2

Amount Per Serving

Calories 457.3 — Calories from Fat 182.8

	% Daily Value *
Total Fat 29.6g	46%
Saturated Fat 19.8g	99%
Cholesterol 372mg	124%
Sodium 146mg	7%
Potassium 567.6mg	17%
Total Carbohydrate 34.2g	12%
Dietary Fiber 3.1g	13%
Sugars 14.8g	
Protein 13.6g	28%

Vitamin A 11.2%	Vitamin C 16.8%
Calcium 4%	Iron 12.2%
Vitamin D 20%	Thiamin 2%
Riboflavin 2%	Vitamin B6 34%
Phosphorus .5%	Magnesium 9.2%

Percent Daily Values are based on a 2,000 calorie diet. Your daily value may be higher or lower depending on your calorie needs.

Fried Egg

Serving: ₡412.91 ≈ $0.69

Gluten Free

Fried Eggs are an easy way to add some protein to your diet. They also make an affordable breakfast, lunch or dinner and work great for a Fried Egg Sandwich. Fried eggs are satiating, so they help you feel full fast, so you don't have to eat a bunch to feel satisfied.

Fried eggs make great snacks too. It only takes a few minutes to fry up an egg, leaving you plenty of time to get back to your activities. Eggs are accepted on many diets and eating plans. We use coconut oil to fry our eggs, as it provides healthier fats. It also has other health benefits, making it a better option over vegetable oil or butter.

Fried Egg

YIELDS
1 Serving

PREP TIME
3 mins

COOK TIME
7 mins

TOTAL TIME
10 mins

Ingredients

- ☐ 1 Tbsp Coconut Oil
- ☐ 2 Eggs
- ☐ 2 dashes Black Pepper

Cook

1. Coat the bottom of a pan with coconut oil and heat on medium-high heat (approximately setting 6.5).

2. Once the pan is hot, crack the eggs into the pan and add pepper.

Tip: If you like over easy eggs, chill the eggs in the refrigerator. This helps the yokes hold their form and not burst when cracking in the pan.

3. Fry the eggs for 1-2 minutes, or until the edges pull away from the pan. Flip and fry for an additional 1-2 minutes.

4. Remove from the pan and serve.

Nutrition Facts

Serving Size 2 Eggs
Servings 1

Amount Per Serving

Calories 246.8   Calories from Fat 90.8

	% Daily Value *
Total Fat 19.6g	**31%**
Saturated Fat 11.5g	**58%**
Cholesterol 372mg	**124%**
Sodium 143mg	**6%**
Potassium 199.2mg	**6%**
Total Carbohydrate 3.8g	**2%**
Dietary Fiber 1.2g	**5%**
Sugars .4g	
Protein 12.4g	**25%**

Vitamin A 10%	Calcium 6%
Iron 10%	Vitamin D 20%
Vitamin B6 10%	Magnesium 2%

Percent Daily Values are based on a 2,000 calorie diet. Your daily value may be higher or lower depending on your calorie needs.

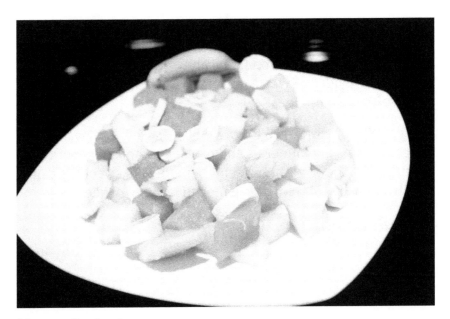

Fruit Salad

Cost Per-Meal: ₡1,182 ≈ $1.97

Serving: ₡591 ≈ $0.99

Vegan

Gluten-free

Fruit salad is a great snack and side! Why not make a large batch, for a quick grab out of the refrigerator? This way you can have a healthy, quick snack, or an instant side dish, and it's a great way to add color and sweetness. Most people don't eat the daily-recommended amount of fruit and often opt for other unhealthy snacks.. However, if you have fruit salad already pre-pared, odds are you will eat more fruit.

When preparing meals, most people focus primarily on the main course. By having pre-prepped food options such as fruit salad, makes it easy to provide healthy snacks and sides. Fruit is natures candy and often cures those sweet tooth cravings It is also a much better option than candy or other sugary snacks. Fruit also provides a sweet contrast to the main course and other salty or spicy sides.

Fruit Salad works well for breakfast, as well. It is packed full of vitamins and minerals and provides a boost of energy to start the day. Along with its health benefits, the sweet taste of fruit beautifully compliments a morning cup of coffee.

Fruit Salad

YIELDS
2 Servings

PREP TIME
10 mins

Ingredients

- ☐ 2 Small Bananas

- ☐ ¾ cup Watermelon

- ☐ 1 cup Pineapple (1/4 of the fruit)

- ☐ 1 cup Mango (approximately 1/2 of the fruit - chopped 5 oz.)

Preparation

1. Cut the fruit into chunks and add to a bowl.

2. Mix the fruit, then place it in individual bowls and serve.

Nutrition Facts

Serving Size 1.5

Servings 2

Amount Per Serving

Calories 201　　　　　　　　　　　　　　　　　　　　　Calories from Fat 1

% Daily Value *

Total Fat .2g	**1%**
Saturated Fat 3.7g	**19%**
Trans Fat 576.8g	
Cholesterol 50.9mg	**17%**
Sodium 5.1mg	**1%**
Protein 2.7g	**6%**

Vitamin A 43.9%	Vitamin C 203.3%
Calcium 3.3%	Iron 3.8%
Vitamin B6 24.1%	Magnesium 10.3%

Percent Daily Values are based on a 2,000 calorie diet. Your daily value may be higher or lower depending on your calorie needs.

Gallo Pinto – Beans & Rice

Cost Per-Meal: ₡1,264.75 ≈ $2.11

Serving: ₡316.19 ≈ $0.53

Vegan   Gluten Free

Gallo Pinto is a Costa Rican classic and the typical side and breakfast dish of Costa Rica. Directly translated it means "spotted rooster." You can see where the color resembles that of the barnyard bird. The vibrant colors of the vegetables and spices contrast those of the rice and beans creating a visually stimulating dish. It is enough to get your mouth watering. And that's before the aroma entices your nose.

The best gallo pinto uses rice and beans that were cooked at least one day before. The locals will often make batches of beans and rice for sides to their casado (typical Costa Rican dish) and use the leftovers to make gallo pinto for breakfast. It seems that the time allows the flavors of the beans to mature and the rice to firm up a bit. Although it takes a few days to prepare this dish, it is delicious.

Note: Many recipes call for lard, but we substitute coconut oil instead, as it's a healthier option. Coconut oil provides the necessary fats, while also adding great flavor.

Gallo Pinto – Beans & Rice

YIELDS
4 Servings

PREP TIME
5 mins

COOK TIME
25 mins

TOTAL TIME
30 mins

Ingredients

- [ ] 2 cups Cooked Beans (red, black or mixed)
- [ ] 5 ½ cups Cooked Rice
- [ ] 1 Tbsp Coconut Oil
- [ ] 3 Clove Garlic
- [ ] 1 Tbsp Fresh Cilantro
- [ ] 2 Small Onion (1 Cup chopped Onion)
- [ ] 1 Sweet Pepper (green, yellow, or red)
- [ ] 1 Tbsp Lizano Sauce

Preparation

1. Chop the sweet pepper and onion and set aside.

2. Mince the clove of garlic and cilantro and set aside.

Cook

3. Coat the bottom of a medium-size skillet with coconut oil over medium heat, (approximately setting 6)

4. When the pan is hot, add half of the minced garlic and half of the onion and sauté.

5. Add beans and rice to the pan, and cook for one minute.

6. Add the peppers, cilantro, remaining onions, and Lizano Salsa to the pan, and cook for five minutes, stirring occasionally.

7. Plate the gallo pinto, serve and enjoy.

Nutrition Facts

Serving Size 1.25 Cup
Servings 4

Amount Per Serving

Calories 255.7   Calories from Fat 92.9

	% Daily Value *
Total Fat 10.8g	**17%**
Saturated Fat 8.3g	**42%**
Trans Fat 193.2g	
Potassium 292mg	**9%**
Total Carbohydrate 33.2g	**12%**
Dietary Fiber 3.9g	**16%**
Sugars 3.0g	
Protein 6.4g	**13%**

Vitamin A 1.2%	Vitamin C 6.3%
Calcium 4%	Iron 12.6%
Vitamin K 2%	Thiamin 13%
Riboflavin 6%	Niacin 4%
Vitamin B6 65.4%	Pantothenic Acid 6%
Phosphorus 15%	Magnesium 9.4%
Zinc 8%	Selenium 20%
Copper 15%	Manganese 84%

Percent Daily Values are based on a 2,000 calorie diet. Your daily value may be higher or lower depending on your calorie needs.

Hardboiled Eggs

Kilo: ₡2,080 ≈ $3.47

Serving: ₡69.33 ≈ $0.12

Gluten Free

Hardboiled eggs are a great snack and also a great topping to salads, sandwiches and more. Eggs offer protein and healthy fats and provide a variety of healthy nutrients for your body. Hardboiled eggs are considered to be a satiating food and therefore help curb cravings and leave you feeling satisfied. Why not add hardboiled eggs to your lunch, serve them as a side, or eat them as a snack for a boost of nutrients and energy

They are also a better option than reaching for that candy bar or bag of chips. Your body will thank you.

Health benefits of hardboiled eggs include:

1. Helps Provide Healthy Cholesterol – Eggs are a healthy cholesterol option. It is true eggs are high in cholesterol, but that doesn't mean it raises the cholesterol in your blood. Your liver simply produces less.

2. Raises HDL (The "Good") Cholesterol – Eggs have high-density lipoprotein levels, which means they raise your HDL level, the good cholesterol.

3. Builds Cell Membranes – Egss are high in choline, a water-soluble vitamin-like essential nutrient, which helps build cell membranes.

4. Helps lower the risk of heart disease. – It has been shown that eggs help lower the risk of heart disease, as they help change small, dense LDL particles to large LDL.

5. Helps With Eye health.- Eggs help contribute to good eye health, as they contain powerful the antioxidants lutein and zeaxanthin.

6. Help Lower Triglycerides – Eggs contain Omega-3 fatty acids, which help lower triglycerides.

7. Helps Builds Tissues and Molecules In The Body – Eggs contain a good dose of quality protein and amino acids, which helps build tissue and molecules in the body.

8. Good Source Of Cholesterol.- Eggs are a source of good cholesterol for your body.

9. Helps With Weight Loss – Eggs contain a variety of macronutrients that are a satiating, so they may help with weight loss

*Healthline

Hardboiled Eggs

YIELDS
1 Serving

COOK TIME
20 mins

TOTAL TIME
20 mins

Ingredients

- [ ] Water
- [ ] 6 Eggs

Cook

10. Fill a pan with water.

11. Add the eggs to the water and bring to boil.

12. Allow the eggs to boil for twenty minutes.

Cool

13. After boiling for twenty minutes, drain the water and run cold water over the eggs for approximately three minutes, or until the eggs feel cool.

14. Crack open the eggs and enjoy! Store unused eggs in the refrigerator for later.

Nutrition Facts

Serving Size 1 egg

Servings 1

Amount Per Serving

Calories 78

	% Daily Value *
Total Fat 5g	8%
Saturated Fat 1.6g	8%
Cholesterol 186.5mg	63%
Sodium 62mg	3%
Potassium 63mg	2%
Total Carbohydrate .6g	1%
Sugars .6g	
Protein 6g	12%

Vitamin A 5%	Calcium 2%
Iron 3%	Vitamin D 10%
Vitamin B6 5%	Magnesium 1%

Percent Daily Values are based on a 2,000 calorie diet. Your daily value may be higher or lower depending on your calorie needs.

Quick Easy Beans and Rice with Egg

Cost Per-Meal: ₡788.98 ≈ $1.31

Serving: ₡394.49 ≈ $0.66

Gluten Free

Quick Easy Beans and Rice with Egg is one of Nikki's favorite lunches. This simple recipe takes under 15 minutes to prepare and is another satiating option. One bowl of Quick Easy Beans and Rice with Egg and you will have the energy to power through your afternoon. The egg compliments the beans and rice nicely, giving it additional flavor and color. Nikki prefers her egg over easy with hot sauce, which adds a zesty flavor to the bowl.

Quick Easy Beans and Rice with Egg

YIELDS
2 Servings

PREP TIME
5 mins

COOK TIME
15 mins

TOTAL TIME
20 mins

Ingredients

- ☐ 2 Tbsp Coconut Oil
- ☐ 1 cup Cooked Beans
- ☐ 1 cup Cooked Rice
- ☐ 2 Eggs
- ☐ 1 Clove Garlic
- ☐ 1 Small Onion

Preparation

1. Coat a medium-sized pan with coconut 1 Tbsp oil and heat over medium-high heat (approximately setting 6).

2. Chop onion

3. Mince garlic

Cook

4. Once the pan is hot, add the onion and garlic and sauté until onions are caramelized and become translucent (approximately two minutes).

5. Add the beans and cook for approximately one minute. Add approximately 1 Tbsp of water to the pan with the fried beans and then add the rice.

6. While the rice and beans are frying, coat a second medium-sized pan with 1 Tbsp coconut oil (enough to coat pan). Heat over medium-high heat (approximately setting 6.5).

7. While the pan is warming up, stir the rice and beans. Cook another 1-2 more minutes or until hot.

8. Once the pan is hot, crack one of the eggs into the pan and fry for 30 seconds to 1 minute, or until the egg turns white.

Tip: If you're having problems with the yoke breaking, place the eggs in the refrigerator for one hour before cooking. Repeat the process with the second egg.

9. Turn the egg over and cook for an additional 20 seconds. If you like your eggs runny (over easy) cook for only 15 seconds after flipping.

10. Repeat with 2nd egg.

11. Once the rice and beans are hot, dish a cup into each bowl and top with the fried egg.

Nutrition Facts

Serving Size 1
Servings 2

Calories 595.4   Calories from Fat 364.4

	% Daily Value *
Total Fat 44.7g	**69%**
Saturated Fat 34.7g	**174%**
Cholesterol 186mg	**62%**
Sodium 75.5mg	**4%**
Potassium 290.4mg	**9%**
Total Carbohydrate 33.6g	**12%**
Dietary Fiber 2.9g	**12%**
Sugars 1.6g	
Protein 11.3g	**23%**

Vitamin A 5.4%	Vitamin C 5.3%
Calcium 5.1%	Iron 12.8%
Vitamin D 10%	Vitamin K 1.3%
Thiamin 8.7%	Riboflavin 4%
Niacin 2.7%	Vitamin B6 50.3%
Pantothenic Acid 4%	Phosphorus 10%
Magnesium 8.4%	Zinc 5.3%
Selenium 13.3%	Copper 10%
Manganese 56%	

Percent Daily Values are based on a 2,000 calorie diet. Your daily value may be higher or lower depending on your calorie needs.

Lunch

el Almuerzo

Chicken Soup – Electric Pressure Cooker

Cost Per-Meal: ₡4,627.99 ≈ $7.71

Serving: ₡1,157.00 ≈ $1.93

Gluten-free

Chicken Soup is not only for when you are sick, but makes a great lunch, dinner or even a quick snack. Using the electric pressure cooker makes it easy to prepare chicken soup for a large family, or banquet.

Once the pot of soup is made, it is simple to reheat a bowl for a fast meal. Loaded with vegetables and chicken, this dish provides many vitamins and minerals your body needs every day. The variety of flavors and textures are very satiating and leave you feeling great. Grab a bowl for lunch, and you'll have plenty of energy to push through your hectic afternoon schedule.

Tip: The recipe can easily be altered to different tastes by selecting a different soup mix flavor.

We used Maggi's "Sopa Criolla Gallina Con Fideos" for our package of soup mix. The nutrition information includes the nutrients from this flavor.

Chicken Soup – Electric Pressure Cooker

YIELDS	PREP TIME	COOK TIME	TOTAL TIME
4 Servings	7 mins	25 mins	32 mins

Ingredients

- [ ] 1 Chicken Fillet (14 Oz.)
- [ ] 1 Package of Maggi Consomé de pollo Concentrado (chicken stalk)
- [ ] 10 Small Potatoes
- [ ] 1 Package Maggi Soup Mix (Sopa Criolla Gallina Con Fideos)
- [ ] 2 cups Green Beans (approximately 2/3 bag fresh)
- [ ] 1 Carrot
- [ ] 4 Cloves of Garlic
- [ ] 1 Large Chive (1/4 Cup chopped)
- [ ] ½ Tbsp Sprigs of Cilantro
- [ ] 10 cups Water
- [ ] 1 Onion

Preparation

1. Mince the garlic.

2. Chop the onions, green beans, carrot, and chives.

3. Cut the potatoes into quarters.

4. Chop the chicken into bite-size pieces.

Cook

5. Add all the ingredients to the pressure cooker (don't forget the dry ingredient packages).

6. Add the water and set to cook on "Soup" setting.

Note: When you add the water, it should reach approximately 4L. Check the capacity of your pressure cooker. You should allow enough room for the pressure. If necessary, reduce the water to accommodate the pressure cooker specifications.

7. Once the soup is finished cooking, allow it to sit in the pot for an additional 2-3 minutes before releasing the pressure.

8. Fill the bowls with a ladle and enjoy.

Nutrition Facts

Serving Size 3 Cups
Servings 4

Amount Per Serving

Calories 555.76   Calories from Fat 25.6

	% Daily Value *
Total Fat 5.8g	9%
Saturated Fat 1.1g	6%
Cholesterol 85mg	29%
Sodium 826.3mg	35%
Potassium 1943.9mg	56%
Total Carbohydrate 90.4g	31%
Dietary Fiber 13g	52%
Sugars 8.9g	
Protein 42.8g	86%

Vitamin A 242.6%	Vitamin C 160%
Calcium 7.2%	Iron 25.7%
Vitamin E 2.1%	Vitamin K 13.2%
Thiamin 15.8%	Riboflavin 8.1%
Niacin 7.5%	Vitamin B6 132.7%
Folate 3.5%	Pantothenic Acid 8.1%
Phosphorus 15%	Magnesium 31.8%
Zinc 8%	Selenium 20%
Copper 15%	Manganese 84%

Percent Daily Values are based on a 2,000 calorie diet. Your daily value may be higher or lower depending on your calorie needs.

Costa Rica Burritos

Cost Per-Meal: ₡916.63 ≈ $1.55

Serving: ₡458.32 ≈ $0.76

Vegan　　　　　Gluten-free

Costa Rica burritos are a favorite in our house and are made with many common ingredients found in Costa Rica and other Latin American countries. As a result, these burritos are an easy and very affordable meal option for any family. Whether you choose the standard flour tortilla, or the gluten-free corn tortilla, your taste buds will thank you for the satisfying flavors. This Costa Rica version of the burrito includes precooked rice and beans and you can find links to the recipes below.

Tip: For a gluten-free option, use corn tortillas. The corn tortillas are generally smaller and as result, make it harder to roll them. The photo of the folded burritos are made with gluten-free corn tortillas and are held together with a toothpick.

We like to add a dash or two of hot sauce for a bit of spice. The Mango Hot Sauce from Jalapeño's restaurant in Playa Negra is definitely our favorite!

Costa Rica Burritos

YIELDS	PREP TIME	COOK TIME	TOTAL TIME
2 Servings	5 mins	10 mins	15 mins

Ingredients

- [ ] ½ cup Rice (precooked)
- [ ] ½ cup Beans (precooked)
- [ ] 4 Tortillas
- [ ] ½ cup Refried Beans
- [ ] 1 Tbsp Coconut Oil
- [ ] 1 cup Cabbage
- [ ] 2 Tomatoes
- [ ] 2 Onions
- [ ] 1 Tbsp Sour Cream (optional)
- [ ] ½ Tbsp Hot Sauce (optional)
- [ ] 1 Tbsp Lizano Salsa (optional)

Preparation

1. Chop the onions and tomatoes and set aside.

2. Slice the cabbage and set aside. We use a banjo/mandolin slicer to create quick, easy, thin slices.

Cook

3. In a medium-size pan, add the coconut oil and heat on medium high heat (approximately setting 6.5) until warm.

4. Add the precooked rice and beans and reheat until warm.

5. On one half of the tortilla, add a 1/8 cup refried beans and spread.

6. Add the bean and rice mixture on top of the refried beans (approximately 1/8 cup).

7. Put a 1/4 of the vegetables (tomato, onion, cabbage) on top of the bean and rice mixture.

8. Add any sauces and sour cream, if desired.

9. Fold in the sides and roll the burrito starting with the edge containing the ingredients.
   (See the gallery for more images on the rolling process.)

10. Top with the remaining vegetables.

Tip: You can also top it off with hot sauce, Lizano Salsa, and sour cream if desired. We recommend a side of fruit and chips with the burritos.

Nutrition Facts

Serving Size 2 Burritos
Servings 2

Amount Per Serving

Calories 532.8	Calories from Fat 231

% Daily Value *

Total Fat 26g	**40%**
Saturated Fat 19.1g	**96%**
Trans Fat .3g	
Sodium 487.4mg	**21%**
Potassium 547.4mg	**16%**
Total Carbohydrate 62.9g	**21%**
Dietary Fiber 8.3g	**34%**
Sugars 7.2g	
Protein 12.6g	**26%**

Vitamin A 20.5%	Vitamin C 47.7%
Calcium 37.7%	Iron 11.7%
Vitamin E .6%	Vitamin K 2.6%
Thiamin 3.1%	Riboflavin .1%
Niacin 3.2%	Vitamin B6 9.4%
Folate 8%	Vitamin B12 2.5%
Phosphorus 17%	Magnesium 13.2%
Zinc .1%	

Percent Daily Values are based on a 2,000 calorie diet. Your daily value may be higher or lower depending on your calorie needs.

Fried Egg Sandwich

Cost Per-Meal: ₡ 841.14 ≈ $1.40

Serving: ₡420.57 ≈ $0.70

Egg sandwiches are a quick and easy way to prepare a hot lunch. These delicious delights are satiating and although they are fried, they are still fairly nutritious.

Note: Although we prefer white bread, whole grain bread is a healthier choice. There are several bakeries and many super-mercado that offer a wide selection of bread options. For a little variety, you can also substitute a tortilla for the bread.

Fried Egg Sandwich

YIELDS
2 Servings

PREP TIME
5 mins

COOK TIME
6 mins

TOTAL TIME
11 mins

Ingredients

- [ ] 4 Eggs (2 Eggs per sandwich)
- [ ] 4 Pieces of bread
- [ ] 1 Tbsp Coconut Oil (Coat the pan)
- [ ] ½ Slices of Onion (4 Slices each sandwich)
- [ ] ½ Slice of Tomato (4 Slices each sandwich)
- [ ] 1 Tbsp Mayonnaise (1/2 on each sandwich)
- [ ] 1 Tbsp Mustard (1/2 on each sandwich)
- [ ] ¼ tsp Black Pepper (Dash on each)

Prepare

1. Coat the bottom of a pan with coconut oil and heat on medium-high heat (approximately 6.5 setting).

2. Slice the onion and tomato and set aside.

Cook

3. Once the pan is hot, crack the eggs into the pan and add the pepper.

Tip: If you like over easy eggs, chill the eggs in the refrigerator. This helps the yokes hold their form and not burst when cracking in the pan.

4. Fry the eggs for 1-2 minutes, until edges pull away from the pan. Flip and fry for an additional 1-2 minutes.

5. Place the bread on a plate and apply mayonnaise and mustard, if desired.

6. Place the fried eggs on a slice of bread. Top the egg with the tomato and onion and the other slice of bread.

7. Cut in half and serve.

Nutrition Facts

Serving Size 1

Servings 2

Amount Per Serving

Calories 625.5   Calories from Fat 294.8

% Daily Value *

Total Fat 48.6g	**75%**
Saturated Fat 30.5g	**153%**
Trans Fat .1g	
Cholesterol 372.1mg	**125%**
Sodium 610.3mg	**26%**
Potassium 213.3mg	**7%**
Total Carbohydrate 26.8g	**9%**
Dietary Fiber 2.2g	**9%**
Sugars 3.1g	
Protein 17.5g	**35%**

Vitamin A 19%	Vitamin C 5%
Calcium 26.7%	Iron 20.4%
Vitamin D 20%	Vitamin E .2%
Vitamin K .7%	Thiamin 20.2%
Riboflavin 12%	Niacin 12.2%
Vitamin B6 10.8%	Folate 2%
Phosphorus 4.3%	Iodine 16%
Magnesium 4.8%	Zinc 12%

Percent Daily Values are based on a 2,000 calorie diet. Your daily value may be higher or lower depending on your calorie needs.

Tostada with Rice & Beans

Cost Per-Meal: ₡698.32 ≈ $1.16

Serving: ₡349.16 ≈ $0.58

Vegan   Gluten-free

Tostada with Rice & Beans is a very quick and easy lunch that offers great taste and needed nutrients. They are a favorite in our house and are made with many common ingredients found in Costa Rica and other Latin American countries. Tostadas are not only easy to make, but they are also very affordable too. Whether you choose the standard flour tortilla or the gluten-free corn tortilla, your taste buds will thank you for the satisfying flavors. Our version of the tostada includes precooked rice and beans. You can find links to the recipes below.

Tip: For a gluten-free version use corn tortillas.

We enjoy adding a dash or two of hot sauce to add a bit of spice. The Mango Hot Sauce from Jalapeño's restaurant in Playa Negra is definitely our favorite!

Tostada with Rice & Beans

YIELDS	PREP TIME	COOK TIME	TOTAL TIME
2 Servings	4 mins	8 mins	12 mins

Ingredients

- ☐ 2 Tortillas
- ☐ ½ cup White Cabbage
- ☐ 1 Small Tomato
- ☐ ½ cup Beans (Black or Red, precooked)
- ☐ 1 Small Onion
- ☐ ½ cup White Rice (precooked)
- ☐ ½ cup Red/Purple Cabbage
- ☐ 1 Tbsp Lizano Salsa (optional)
- ☐ ½ Tbsp Hot Sauce (optional)
- ☐ 1 Tbsp Sour Cream (optional)

Preparation

1. Chop the onion and tomato and set aside.

2. Slice the cabbage and set aside. We use a banjo/mandolin slicer to create quick, easy, thin slices.

Cook

3. Toast the tortillas in a toaster oven. If you do not have a toaster oven, you can fry your tortillas in a pan.

4. Place the tortilla on a plate and cover with the rice & beans.

Assemble

5. Cover the rice & beans with the onions, tomatoes, and cabbage.

6. Top with hot sauce, Lizano Salsa, and sour cream, if desired.

7. We recommend a side of fruit and chips for the Tostada with Rice & Beans.

Nutrition Facts

Serving Size 1
Servings 2

Amount Per Serving

Calories 217.7   Calories from Fat 14.6

	% Daily Value *
Total Fat 2.6g	4%
Saturated Fat 1.1g	6%
Trans Fat .2g	
Cholesterol 251.1mg	84%
Potassium 422.8mg	13%
Total Carbohydrate 42.3g	15%
Dietary Fiber 6.7g	27%
Sugars 4.1g	
Protein 8.4g	17%

Vitamin A 14.6%	Vitamin C 40.4%
Calcium 21.2%	Iron 13.3%
Vitamin E .3%	Vitamin K 1.8%
Thiamin 3.6%	Riboflavin 1.6%
Niacin 1.4%	Vitamin B6 20.8%
Folate 4%	Pantothenic Acid 1.5%
Phosphorus 12.3%	Magnesium 10.4%
Zinc 2.1%	Selenium 5%
Copper 3.8%	Manganese 21%

Percent Daily Values are based on a 2,000 calorie diet. Your daily value may be higher or lower depending on your calorie needs.

200

Dinner:

la Cena

Chicken & Camote – Electric Pressure Cooker

Cost Per-Meal: ₡1915.03 ≈ $3.19

Serving: ₡957.52 ≈ $1.60

Gluten Free

Chicken & Camote - Electric pressure cooker is another quick and easy recipe that produces a very nutritious meal. Not only is Chicken & Camote - Electric pressure cooker packed with nutrients, but is extremely affordable too! Camote is sweet, so it compliments the savory flavors of the chicken perfectly.

Chicken & Camote – Electric Pressure Cooker

YIELDS
2 Servings

PREP TIME
5 mins

COOK TIME
35 mins

TOTAL TIME
40 mins

Ingredients

- [ ] 1 Chicken Fillet 7oz.
- [ ] 2 Camote
- [ ] 1 Small Onion
- [ ] ½ tsp Cilantro
- [ ] 2 Cloves of Garlic
- [ ] ½ tsp Oregano
- [ ] ⅛ tsp Salt
- [ ] ¼ tsp Black Pepper

Preparation

1. Place the whole piece in the electric pressure cooker.

2. Mince garlic cloves and top the chicken.

3. Chop the onion and top the chicken.

4. Sprinkle the dry seasoning evenly over the chicken.

5. Peel the camote. If it's a large piece, cut it in half. Once peeled, place the pieces immediately into ice water until you are ready to start cooking.

Note: Camote will turn brown/black rapidly once it is peeled. If you don't like the look, place camote in the refrigerator until cold. Once peeled pieces immediately into ice water until you are ready to start cooking.

Cook

6. Place the lid on the pot and cook on the "Poultry" setting.

7. When finished cooking, release the pressure, remove the lid, and take out the chicken.

8. Cut the chicken in half and place on the plates.

9. Then plate the remaining vegetables.

Tip: We recommend adding a bright colored slaw, or fruit salad to increase the visual presentation of the dish.

Nutrition Facts

Serving Size 1
Servings 2

Amount Per Serving

Calories 460.1 | Calories from Fat .1

	% Daily Value *
Total Fat 7.6g	12%
Saturated Fat 2g	10%
Cholesterol 170mg	57%
Sodium 366.9mg	16%
Potassium 500.4mg	15%
Total Carbohydrate 30.1g	11%
Dietary Fiber 4.7g	19%
Sugars 6.3g	
Protein 64.6g	130%

Vitamin A 368.6%	Vitamin C 10.3%
Calcium 4.6%	Iron 7.2%
Vitamin K 2%	Thiamin 13%
Riboflavin 6%	Niacin 4%
Vitamin B6 78.5%	Pantothenic Acid 6%
Phosphorus 15%	Magnesium 14.6%
Zinc 8%	Selenium 20%
Copper 15%	Manganese 84%

Percent Daily Values are based on a 2,000 calorie diet. Your daily value may be higher or lower depending on your calorie needs.

Chicken & Chayote – Electric Pressure Cooker

Cost Per-Meal: ₡1,75.56 $1.79

Serving: ₡268.89 $0.45

Gluten-free

Chicken & Chayote - Electric Pressure Cooker is another simple pressure cooker recipe. The electric pressure cooker does a great job of sealing in the moisture and flavor of the chicken and the chayote. The seasonings are drawn into the meat and vegetables, providing great flavor and juicy tender bites.

Minimal preparation and cook time make this a great option for nights you have plans and little time to cook. Both chicken and chayote are plentiful in Central America making this dish an affordable option. Cheap, easy, and nutritious what more could you ask for?

Note: Nutrition information does not include sauce.

Chicken & Chayote – Electric Pressure Cooker

YIELDS
4 Servings

PREP TIME
5 mins

COOK TIME
35 mins

TOTAL TIME
40 mins

Ingredients

- [ ] 4 Chicken Fillet (3.5 ounce each)
- [ ] 2 Small Onion
- [ ] 2 Cloves of Garlic
- [ ] 4 Chayote
- [ ] 1 tsp Paprika
- [ ] ½ tsp Thyme
- [ ] 1 Tomato
- [ ] 4 Tbsp Mayonnaise (Optional-Dipping sauce)
- [ ] 4 dashes Hot Sauce - to taste (Optional-Dipping sauce)
- [ ] ½ Lime (Optional-Dipping sauce)

Preparation

1. Chop the onion and place half in one small bowl for the seasoning mixture. Place the other half in a separate small bowl, and set it aside.

2. Mince the garlic, and add it to the seasoning bowl.

3. Combine the thyme and paprika to the seasoning bowl, and set it aside.

4. Chop the tomato and add it to the onions (NOT the seasoning mix) then set it aside.

5. Peel the chayote. Cut the chayote in half down the crease. Use a spoon to remove the seed. Cut each piece in half again to create quarters.

Cook

6. Place the whole piece in the electric pressure cooker.

7. Top the chicken with half of the contents of the seasoning bowl.

8. Place the chayote pieces on top of the seasoned chicken. Top the chayote with the remaining contents of the seasoning bowl.

9. Secure the lid to the pot, and start on the "Poultry" setting.

10. When finished cooking, release the pressure and remove the lid.

11. Take the chicken from the electric pressure cooker, and cut it in half. Place a piece of chicken and chayote on plates.

12. Top the chicken with the onion and tomato mixture and serve.

Prepare Dipping Sauce For Chayote (Optional)

13. Squeeze the lime half into a small bowl.

14. Mix in the mayonnaise and hot sauce.

15. Spoon the sauce into small dipping bowls, or directly onto plates.

Nutrition Facts

Serving Size 1
Servings 4

Amount Per Serving

Calories 131.2   Calories from Fat .1

	% Daily Value *
Total Fat 5.5g	9%
Saturated Fat 1.7g	9%
Trans Fat .1g	
Cholesterol 186mg	62%
Sodium 105.8mg	5%
Potassium 433.5mg	13%
Total Carbohydrate 13.9g	5%
Dietary Fiber 4.8g	20%
Sugars 5.6g	
Protein 8.4g	17%

Vitamin A 15.6%	Vitamin C 33.7%
Calcium 14.4%	Iron 9.3%
Vitamin D 10%	Vitamin E .2%
Vitamin K 1.7%	Thiamin 6.7%
Riboflavin 3%	Niacin 2.2%
Vitamin B6 47.5%	Folate 2%
Pantothenic Acid 3%	Phosphorus 11.8%
Magnesium 13.4%	Zinc 4%
Selenium 10%	Copper 7.5%
Manganese 42%	

Percent Daily Values are based on a 2,000 calorie diet. Your daily value may be higher or lower depending on your calorie needs.

Crispy Breaded Fried Chicken

Cost Per-Meal: ₡2,856.20≈ $5.36

Serving: ₡1,428.10 ≈ $2.68

If you're looking for a taste of home, with a bit of a new home feel, try this breaded fried chicken recipe. The coconut oil will give a hint of tropical flavor, along with the crispy chicken strips you remember from back home. For a cheaper option, you can use lard in place of the coconut oil. It will, however, give it a slightly different taste.

Note:

-Nutrition information reflects 1/4 cup white flour. This is to account for the amount on the chicken, not including the excess left on the plate.

-You can also substitute Gluten free flour.

-Nutrition information reflects 1 cup of Coconut oil, as there will be oil left over in the pan.

Crispy Breaded Fried Chicken

YIELDS
2 Servings

PREP TIME
7 mins

COOK TIME
25 mins

TOTAL TIME
32 mins

Ingredients

- ☐ 2 Chicken Fillet (3.5 ounce each)
- ☐ 1 Small Onion
- ☐ ½ tsp Salt
- ☐ 1 cup Flour
- ☐ ½ tsp Black Pepper
- ☐ ½ tsp Rosemary
- ☐ 1 Clove Garlic
- ☐ 2 cups Coconut Oil
- ☐ 2 Eggs

Preparation

1. Add the coconut oil to the pan and heat on medium-high heat (approximately 6.5 setting).

2. Chop the onion, and mince the garlic, and set aside.

3. Crack the eggs into a bowl. Whisk with them with a fork, until eggs are mixed.

4. Slice the chicken into roughly 3/4 - inch strips.

5. Measure the flour, salt, rosemary, and pepper on a plate, and mix with a fork.

6. Place the pieces of chicken, one at a time, in the eggs and thoroughly coat.

7. Take the egg coated chicken pieces, and roll them one at a time in the flour, until they are covered.

Cook

8. When the oil in the pan is hot, place the coated chicken in the pan, leaving at least 1/2 inch space between pieces.

9. Let the chicken cook in the oil for approximately three minutes and then flip.

10. After you flip the chicken pieces, add the onions and garlic to the pan.

11. After the second side of the chicken has cooked for three minutes, alternate sides by flipping every one to two minutes, until both sides are golden brown in color.

Note: Do not forget to flip the chicken pieces regularly, or they will burn on the outside, and inside may be raw.

12. When the chicken pieces are golden brown on both sides, remove the chicken from the pan and place it on a paper towel covered plate. Let the chicken pieces sit for a few minutes to allow the paper towel to absorb the excess grease.

13. Plate the chicken with your favorite sides and serve.

We recommend a slaw salad and piece of fruit.
(Pictured: Mango Slaw Salad and a piece of watermelon.)

Nutrition Facts

Serving Size 1
Servings 2

Amount Per Serving

Calories 3326 | Calories from Fat 2904

	% Daily Value *
Total Fat 322.3g	496%
Saturated Fat 267.1g	1336%
Cholesterol 313.5mg	105%
Sodium 763.7mg	32%
Potassium 116.8mg	4%
Total Carbohydrate 23g	8%
Dietary Fiber 1.3g	6%
Sugars .2g	
Protein 55.6g	112%

Vitamin A 5.3%	Vitamin C .3%
Calcium 2.8%	Iron 12.3%
Vitamin D 10%	Thiamin 10%
Riboflavin 6%	Niacin 8%
Vitamin B6 5%	Folate 10%
Magnesium 1%	

Percent Daily Values are based on a 2,000 calorie diet. Your daily value may be higher or lower depending on your calorie needs.

Fried Spaghetti

Cost Per-Meal: ₡729.76 ≈ $1.22

Serving: ₡364.88 ≈ $0.61

Vegan

If you are looking for a light meal that really hits the spot, make sure you try this Fried Spaghetti. It works great for a quick, easy dinner or lunch. It is also a great alternative to standard boiled noodles with sauce. The fried spaghetti noodles offer a different texture and the fresh tomatoes and onions top it off nicely, to complete the dish.

Fried Spaghetti

YIELDS
2 Servings

PREP TIME
3 mins

COOK TIME
25 mins

TOTAL TIME
28 mins

Ingredients

- [ ] Water
- [ ] 1 ½ Tbsp Coconut Oil
- [ ] 3 Cloves Garlic
- [ ] 1 Tbsp Fresh Oregano
- [ ] 1 Tomato
- [ ] 3.9oz Spaghetti Noodles (see noodle package for serving size)
- [ ] 1 ½ Onion
- [ ] ½ tsp Salt
- [ ] ½ tsp pepper

Preparation

1. Begin by filling a pot with water. Add 1/2 Tbsp coconut oil and bring to a boil.

2. While the water warms, mince the garlic and the oregano.

3. Chop the tomato and the onion.

Cook

4. Once the water comes to a boil, add the noodles and allow to boil for seven to ten minutes, or until desired softness. You may want to stir every couple minutes to help keep the noodles from sticking together. (Check the noodle packaging for more specific information.)

5. With approximately 3 minutes remaining on the noodles, coat the bottom of a pan with 1 Tbsp coconut oil. Heat the pan on medium-high heat (approximately setting 6.5).

6. Sauté 1/2 of the garlic and 1/3 of the onions, until onions are caramelized and become translucent (approximately two minutes).

7. When finished boiling, drain the water from the noodles.

8. Once the onions are caramelized, add 1/2 the tomato, oregano, salt, and pepper to the pan and begin frying.

9. After 30 seconds, stir the tomatoes, and then add the spaghetti noodles to the pan. Fry for 1 minute, stirring often to reduce sticking.

10. Add 1/2 of the remaining onions to the pan. Continue to fry for the remaining 1-2 minutes, depending on desired crispiness of the noodles.

11. Remove from heat and place the noodles on plates. Top the noodles with the remaining onions and tomatoes.

Nutrition Facts

Serving Size 1
Servings 2

Amount Per Serving

Calories 510.6	Calories from Fat 281.4

	% Daily Value *
Total Fat 30.7g	**48%**
Saturated Fat 24.8g	**124%**
Trans Fat .2g	
Sodium 642mg	**27%**
Potassium 187mg	**6%**
Total Carbohydrate 47.7g	**16%**
Dietary Fiber 4.7g	**19%**
Sugars 4.2g	
Protein 8.4g	**17%**

Vitamin A 10%	Vitamin C 14.1%
Calcium 21.3%	Iron 14.4%
Vitamin E .3%	Vitamin K 4.3%
Thiamin 49.8%	Riboflavin 19.1%
Niacin 21.4%	Vitamin B6 95.3%
Folate 34%	Pantothenic Acid 9%
Phosphorus 31%	Magnesium 14.9%
Zinc 12.1%	Selenium 30%
Copper 22.5%	Manganese 126%

Percent Daily Values are based on a 2,000 calorie diet. Your daily value may be higher or lower depending on your calorie needs.

Pan Fried Chicken Strips – Gluten-free

Cost Per-Meal: ₡2240.29 ≈ $3.73

Serving: ₡560.07 ≈ $0.93

Gluten-free

These Pan Fried Chicken Strips - Gluten-free are made with coconut oil to seal in the juicy flavors. This dish is easy to make, and one of our children's favorites. By using coconut oil instead of vegetable oil or other lard type options, this recipe provides healthy fats with great Costa Rican flavor. Chicken is one of the cheaper proteins available in Costa Rica, and these strips are a great main dish that should fit in your budget.

Pan Fried Chicken Strips – Gluten-free

YIELDS
2 Servings

PREP TIME
10 mins

COOK TIME
15 mins

TOTAL TIME
25 mins

Ingredients

- [ ] 4 Chicken Fillet (3.5 ounce each)
- [ ] ¼ cup Coconut Oil
- [ ] 2 Small Onions
- [ ] 2 Cloves Garlic
- [ ] 1 tsp Black Pepper
- [ ] ¼ tsp Salt
- [ ] ½ tsp Rosemary

Preparation

1. Add the coconut oil to a large frying pan and heat on medium-high heat (approximately setting 6.5)

2. Chop the onions and mince the garlic.

3. Slice the chicken into roughly 3/4-inch strips.

4. Sprinkle the salt, pepper, and rosemary evenly over the chicken pieces.

Cook

5. Once the pan is hot, add the onion and garlic. Allow caramelizing for approximately 2-3 minutes. Onions will become translucent.

Note: Do not burn the onion and garlic. It is better to err on too little than too much.

6. Place the seasoned chicken in the pan with the caramelized onions and garlic and cook for about 2-1/2 minutes.

7. Flip the chicken in the pan and fry for an additional 2-1/2 minutes.

8. Continue frying and flipping in 2-minute increments, until both sides are golden brown, approximately 8-10 minutes total fry time.

9. Once the chicken pieces are golden brown on both sides, remove the chicken from the pan, and place it on a paper towel covered plate. Let the chicken pieces sit for a few minutes to allow the paper towel to absorb the excess grease.

10. Plate the chicken with your favorite sides and serve.

Tip: We recommend a slaw salad and piece of fruit.

(Pictured: Mango Slaw Salad, and a piece of watermelon).

Nutrition Facts

Serving Size 1
Servings 4

Amount Per Serving

Calories 544.3   Calories from Fat 363.1

	% Daily Value *
Total Fat 43g	67%
Saturated Fat 34g	170%
Cholesterol 85mg	29%
Sodium 221mg	10%
Potassium 57.5mg	2%
Total Carbohydrate 3.7g	2%
Dietary Fiber .8g	4%
Sugars 1.3g	
Protein 31.5g	63%

Vitamin A .1%	Vitamin C 4.5%
Calcium 1.3%	Iron 2%
Vitamin K 1%	Thiamin 6.5%
Riboflavin 3%	Niacin 2%
Vitamin B6 32.5%	Pantothenic Acid 3%
Phosphorus 7.5%	Magnesium 3.6%
Zinc 4%	Selenium 10%
Copper 7.5%	Manganese 42%

Percent Daily Values are based on a 2,000 calorie diet. Your daily value may be higher or lower depending on your calorie needs.

Pan Fried Pineapple Pork Steak

Cost Per-Meal: ₡3,103.43 ≈ $5.17

Serving: ₡1,551.71 ≈ $2.59

Gluten-free

Pan Fried Pineapple Pork Steak is a delicious and affordable meat dish. If you are looking for a low-cost alternative to chicken, this dish hits the spot. Pineapple compliments the pan-fried pork steak perfectly with its juicy sweetness and bright color. The flavor and spices penetrate to the center of the meat by marinating the meat overnight. At under $3 per person, pan-fried pineapple pork steak is a savory main course that will keep you on budget.

Pan Fried Pineapple Pork Steak

YIELDS
2 Servings

PREP TIME
10 mins

COOK TIME
10 mins

TOTAL TIME
20 mins

Ingredients

- [ ] ½ kg Pork Steak - Bistec de Cerdo
- [ ] ¼ cup Lizano
- [ ] 1 Medium onion
- [ ] ½ tsp Pepper
- [ ] 3 Cloves garlic
- [ ] ½ tbsp Cilantro
- [ ] 4 tbsp Coconut Oil (enough to coat the bottom of a big pan)
- [ ] ¼ cup Chopped pineapple.

Preparation

1. Chop the onion.

2. Mince the garlic and cilantro.

3. Place the pork steak in a container with a lid.

Tip: We try to limit single-use plastic so we use washable container. However, you can use a ziplock bag for easy disposals.

4. Cover pork steak with Lizano.

Tip: You can place the lid on the bowl and shake to help cover.

5. Sprinkle onions, garlic, and cilantro covering both sides of the pork steak. Place the lid on bowl and shake to

coat.

6. Place sealed container in the refrigerator overnight.

Cook

7. Coat the bottom of a big pan with coconut oil. Heat on medium-high heat (approximately 6.5 setting).

8. When the oil in the pan is hot, place the pork steak in the pan. Scrape out the remaining sauce and seasoning onto the pork steak.

9. Let the pork steak cook in the oil for approximately three minutes and then flip.

10. After the second side of the pork steak has cooked for three and a half minutes, flipping and cook for an additional one and a half minutes.

Note: Cook time can vary depending on the thickness of pork steak.

11. Remove the pork steak from the pan and plate.

12. Top the pork steak with chopped pineapple and serve.

Nutrition Facts

Serving Size 1
Servings 2

Amount Per Serving

Calories 1246.6   Calories from Fat 726.2

	% Daily Value *
Total Fat 106.7g	**165%**
Saturated Fat 66g	**330%**
Cholesterol 160.6mg	**54%**
Sodium 120.3mg	**6%**
Potassium 689.2mg	**20%**
Total Carbohydrate 18g	**6%**
Dietary Fiber 1.7g	**7%**
Sugars 12.5g	
Protein 44.9g	**90%**

Vitamin A .8%	Vitamin C 26.1%
Calcium 8.3%	Iron 14.6%
Vitamin D 26%	Vitamin K 3%
Thiamin 19.5%	Riboflavin 9%
Niacin 6%	Vitamin B6 122.3%
Folate 29%	Pantothenic Acid 9%
Phosphorus 22.5%	Magnesium 18.7%
Zinc 12%	Selenium 30%
Copper 22.5%	Manganese 126%

Percent Daily Values are based on a 2,000 calorie diet. Your daily value may be higher or lower depending on your calorie needs.

Pasta & Vegetables In White Sauce

Cost Per-Meal: ₡5,274.32 ≈ $8.79

Serving: ₡2,637.16 ≈ $4.40

Pasta and Vegetables in White Sauce is a delicious dish that incorporates some vegetables that are frequently overlooked. Eggplant and zucchini add flavor and nutrients to this dish along with splashes of color. The bright vegetables and creamy sauce will have your mouth watering anticipating the delicious flavors to come.

Tip: For a gluten-free option, simply replace the standard pasta with a gluten-free variety and cook as instructed.

Pasta & Vegetables In White Sauce

YIELDS
2 Servings

PREP TIME
10 mins

COOK TIME
20 mins

TOTAL TIME
30 mins

Ingredients

- [ ] 6 cups Water
- [ ] ½ Package of Pasta (your preferred type)
- [ ] 1½ Tbsp Coconut Oil (Coat Pan)
- [ ] 1 Tbsp Chives
- [ ] 4 Cloves Garlic
- [ ] 1 Tbsp Oregano
- [ ] ½ Tbsp Cilantro
- [ ] 2 Onions
- [ ] 1 Tomato
- [ ] ½ Eggplant
- [ ] ½ Zucchini
- [ ] 3 cups Cream Dulce or (1 bag of Natilla - Sour Cream)
- [ ] ¾ tsp salt
- [ ] 1 tsp Black Pepper

Preparation

1. Begin by filling a pot with water. Add 1/2 Tbsp coconut oil and bring to a boil.

2. While water warms, mince the garlic, cilantro, chives, and oregano.

3. Chop the eggplant, zucchini, tomato, chives, and onion.

Cook

4. Once the water comes to a boil, add the noodles and allow to boil for seven to ten minutes, or until desired softness. You may want to stir every couple minutes to help keep the noodles from sticking together. (Check the noodle packaging for more specific information).

5. When there are approximately 3 minutes remaining on the noodles, coat the bottom of a pan with 1 Tbsp coconut oil and heat on the stove over medium-high heat (approximately setting 6.5).

6. Sauté 1/2 of the garlic, and 1/3 of the onions until the onions caramelize and become translucent (approximately two minutes).

7. When finished boiling, drain the water from the noodles.

8. Once the onions are caramelized, add 1/3 of the tomato to the pan and begin frying.

9. After 30 seconds, add the eggplant, zucchini, and chives and stir and then fry for 1 minute.

10. Add the pasta noodles, cream, salt, and pepper to the pan and fry for 2-3 minutes, stirring often to reduce sticking.

11. After the pasta and sauce have fried for 1 minute, add 1/3 of the onions to the pan and continue to fry for the remaining 1-2 minutes, depending on desired crispiness of the noodles.

12. Remove from heat and place the noodles on plates. Top the noodles with the remaining onions and tomatoes.

Nutrition Facts

Serving Size 1
Servings 2

Calories 1831.2   Calories from Fat 281.5

% Daily Value *

Total Fat 163.2g	**252%**
Saturated Fat 100.9g	**505%**
Trans Fat .2g	
Sodium 1067.4mg	**45%**
Potassium 671.3mg	**20%**
Total Carbohydrate 74.7g	**25%**
Dietary Fiber 9.7g	**39%**
Sugars 10.8g	
Protein 18.2g	**37%**

Vitamin A 13.9%	Vitamin C 37.3%
Calcium 125.2%	Iron 17.5%
Vitamin E .3%	Vitamin K 5.3%
Thiamin 56.3%	Riboflavin 22.1%
Niacin 23.4%	Vitamin B6 137.1%
Folate 34%	Pantothenic Acid 12%
Phosphorus 38.5%	Magnesium 25%
Zinc 16.1%	Selenium 40%
Copper 30%	Manganese 168%

Percent Daily Values are based on a 2,000 calorie diet. Your daily value may be higher or lower depending on your calorie needs.

Seasoned Chicken & Potatoes – Electric Pressure Cooker

Cost Per-Meal: ₡2713.64 ≈ $4.52

Serving: ₡1356.82 ≈ $2.26

Gluten-free

Seasoned Chicken & Potatoes is a simple, yet delicious Electric pressure cooker recipe. This tasty dish is a great way to add protein and other nutrients to your diet. The electric pressure cooker pressure cooker does a great job trapping the juices of the chicken, resulting in moist flavorful bites. The potatoes are tasty too, since they absorb the spices and flavoring from the chicken. Just add a few garnishes and you have a dish that is appealing and mouthwatering.

Tip: Add hot sauce or other sauce to increase flavor, as desired.

Note: Adding butter to potatoes increases the flavor, but also adds fat and calories

Seasoned Chicken & Potatoes – Electric Pressure Cooker.

YIELDS
1 Serving

PREP TIME
7 mins

COOK TIME
30 mins

TOTAL TIME
37 mins

Ingredients

- [ ] 1 Chicken Fillet 14 oz.
- [ ] 4 Small Potatoes
- [ ] ½ Lime
- [ ] 1 Tomato
- [ ] 2 Small Onions
- [ ] 2 Coves of Garlic
- [ ] ½ tsp Rosemary
- [ ] ½ Tbsp Cilantro

Preparation

1. Place the whole piece in the electric pressure cooker.

2. Zest lime and sprinkle rosemary over the chicken.

3. Chop the onions, and tomatoes, and set aside.

4. Mince the garlic and cilantro.

5. Cover the chicken with the garlic, cilantro, and half of the onions.

6. Add the potatoes to the pot.

Cook

7. Place the lid on the pot and start on the "Chicken" setting.

8. Combine the tomatoes and remaining onion.

9. Once finished cooking, release the pressure, remove chicken and cut in two. Place one piece of chicken and two potatoes on each plate.

10. Top the chicken pieces with tomatoes and onions and serve.

Tip: We recommend serving with a side of Slaw Salad.

Nutrition Facts

Serving Size 2
Servings 1

Amount Per Serving

Calories 632.6

Calories from Fat .1

% Daily Value *

Total Fat 8.3g	13%
Saturated Fat 2g	10%
Trans Fat .2g	
Cholesterol 170mg	57%
Sodium 229.5mg	10%
Potassium 1650.2mg	48%
Total Carbohydrate 70.1g	24%
Dietary Fiber 10.1g	41%
Sugars 6.7g	
Protein 70.2g	141%

Vitamin A 10.9%	Vitamin C 133.5%
Calcium 23.1%	Iron 18.2%
Vitamin E .3%	Vitamin K 3.3%
Thiamin 13.3%	Riboflavin 6.1%
Niacin 4.4%	Vitamin B6 115.1%
Folate 4%	Pantothenic Acid 6%
Phosphorus 23.5%	Magnesium 30.5%
Zinc 8.1%	Selenium 20%
Copper 15%	Manganese 84%

Percent Daily Values are based on a 2,000 calorie diet. Your daily value may be higher or lower depending on your calorie needs.

Stir Fry Garlic Chicken

Cost Per-Meal: ₡1308.16 ≈ $2.18

Serving: ₡654.08 ≈ $1.09

Gluten Free

Another affordable and easy meal is Stir Fry Garlic Chicken. This dish offers a variety of flavors and colors and is simple to make. With a total time of fewer than thirty minutes, this is the perfect meal for those nights when you have little time to cook before the evening's activities. Stir Fry Garlic Chicken offers bright vegetables and juicy chicken pieces that are certain to get your mount watering. In addition, the chicken, garlic, and veggies provide low-fat nutrients that are great for boosting energy and your overall health.

Seasoned Chicken & Potatoes – Electric Pressure Cooker

YIELDS
2 Servings

PREP TIME
8 mins

COOK TIME
18 mins

TOTAL TIME
26 mins

Ingredients

- [ ] 1 Tbsp Coconut Oil
- [ ] 3 Cloves Garlic
- [ ] ¼ cup Cilantro
- [ ] 1 Medium-size Onion
- [ ] 2 Chives
- [ ] 1 Sweet Pepper
- [ ] 1 Chicken Fillet (7oz)

Preparation

1. Coat the bottom of a medium-size frying pan with coconut oil and heat on medium-high (approximately setting 6.5).

2. Mince the garlic and cilantro.

3. Chop the chicken fillet into roughly one-inch bites

4. Chop the sweet pepper, chives, and onion.

Cook

5. Once the pan is hot, add the garlic and cilantro. Allow the garlic and cilantro to cook in the oil for a minute before adding additional ingredients.

6. Add the chicken pieces to the pan with the garlic and cilantro.

7. After the chicken has cooked for two minutes, add the bell pepper, chives, and onion to the pan. Stir occasionally and cook for 10-12 minutes.

8. Plate your dish either in one bowl or on individual plates with sides of choice.

Tip: We recommended green beans, mashed potatoes, and toasted tortilla as sides.

Nutrition Facts

Serving Size 1
Servings 2

Calories 375.3 | Calories from Fat 181.7

	% Daily Value *
Total Fat 23.5g	37%
Saturated Fat 17.6g	89%
Cholesterol 85mg	29%
Sodium 77.5mg	4%
Potassium 151.9mg	5%
Total Carbohydrate 6.5g	3%
Dietary Fiber 1.6g	7%
Sugars 2.5g	
Protein 32.1g	65%

Vitamin A 5.2%	Vitamin C 69.5%
Calcium 1.2%	Iron 2.3%
Vitamin K 3%	Thiamin 19.5%
Riboflavin 9%	Niacin 6%
Vitamin B6 99.5%	Pantothenic Acid 9%
Phosphorus 22.5%	Magnesium 10.6%
Zinc 12%	Selenium 30%
Copper 22.5%	Manganese 126%

Percent Daily Values are based on a 2,000 calorie diet. Your daily value may be higher or lower depending on your calorie needs.

Final Thoughts

Now that you have absorbed the information in this book, you should have an understanding of what it takes to cook in Costa Rica on a budget. Not only will this information help benefit your financial situation, it will also benefit your body, as the recipes provided are nutrient rich. What's more, they should give you a boost of energy, which you can use to experience all the wonders Costa Rica has to offer.

Our hope is that you discovered some valuable information and tips to embark on your journey. We wish to leave you with these blessings:

May your efforts be effective and produce amazing results.

May you overcome the obstacles that block your path to true happiness.

May your lives be ever enriched, as you challenge your current boundaries.

May you experience authentic "Pura Vida."

(Pura vida, literally translated "pure life" is a common greeting and farewell offered in Costa Rica.)

Glossary of Terms

General Spanish Terms

🗣 el Almuerzo: Lunch

🗣 Caja:
1. Register or checkout
2. Box
3. The national health care system administered by the Costarricense de Seguro   Social (CCSS)

🗣 Carnicería: Butcher's shop; these meat shops offer fresh beef, poultry, and pork.

🗣 la Cena: Dinner

🗣 Colón: The currency of Costa Rica with a 2017 value of around ₡570 to $1.

🗣 Cuenta:
1. Count
2. Account
3. Bill
4. Check
5. Total
6. Estimate

🗣 el Desayuno: Breakfast

🗣 Expat: People living in one country with citizenship from another.

🗣 Feria: Fair, market. These markets are open-air areas that may have multiple vendors selling various goods. The term is also used in reference to the festivals that often include a rodeo and carnival.

- Gringo / gringa: A person, especially an American, who is not Hispanic or Latino (male / female)

- Llenar: Spanish word for "fill"

- Mercado: A market. Could be any type of market, but is generally used to indicate the larger stores.

- Mil: 1,000 in Spanish

- Pura vida: Literally translated "pure life" and is a common greeting and farewell offered in Costa Rica

Foods: English to Spanish

Fruit

- Apple – Manzana

- Avocado - Aguacate

- Banana – Banano, Plátano

- Blackberries – Moras

- Blueberries – Arádanos azules

- Cantaloupe – Cantalupo, Melón

- Coconut – Coco

- Coconut Water – Agua de coco, Pipa fria (Usually served in the coconut.)

- Green Coconut – Pipa, Coco verde

- Fruit – Fruta

- Grapefruit – Pomelo

- Grapes – Uvas

- Green Grapes – Uvas verdes
- Purple Grapes – Uvas moradas
- Seedless Grapes – Uvas sin semillas
- Guava – Guayaba
- Kiwi - Kiwi
- Lime – Limón
- Mandarin Lime – Limón mandarino
- Mango – Mango
- Nectarine - Nectarina
- Orange – Naranja
- Papaya – Papaya
- Passion Fruit – Maracuyá, Granadilla
- Peach – Melocotón
- Pear – Pera
- Pineapple – Piña
- Plantain – Plátano
- Green, Plantain – Verde, plátano
- Rambutan – Mamón chino
- Raspberries – Frambuesas
- Soursop – Guanábana
- Star Fruit – Carambola, Fruta estrella
- Strawberries – Fresas
- Tangerina - mandarina

- Water Apple – Manzana de agua

- Watermelon – Sandía

- Tomatoes - Los tomates

Vegetables

- Artichoke – Alcachofa

- Asparagus - Espárragos

- Bell Pepper – Chile morrón, Pimiento

- Broccoli – Brócoli

- Brussels Sprouts – Coles de bruselas

- Button Mushroom – Botón de setas

- Cabbage, Green – Repollo verde

- Cabbage, Purple – Repollo morado

- Carrot – Zanahoria

- Cauliflower – Coliflor

- Celery – Apio

- Corn – Maíz

- Corn on the Cob – Maíz en la mazorca

- Corn, Sweet – Maíz dulce

- Cucumber – Pepino

- Eggplant – Berenjena

- Garlic – Ajo

- Green Beans – Vainica, Judías verdes
- Hot Chile Pepper – Chile picante, Pimienta de chili caliente
- Jalapeño – Chile jalapeño
- Kale – Col rizada
- Leek – Puerro
- Lettuce – Lechuga
- Lettuce, Iceberg – Lechuga iceberg
- Lettuce, Romaine – Lechuga romana
- Lima Beans – Frijoles de lima
- Mushrooms – Hongos
- Onion – Cebolla
- Potato- La papa, Patata
- Prunes – Ciruelas
- Pumpkin – Calabaza
- Purple Onion – Cebolla morada
- Scallion – Cebollino
- Shallots – Echalotes, Chalotes
- Sweet Potato
- Spinach – Espinacas
- Sprouts – Coles
- Squash – Squash
- Sweet Pepper – Chile dulce, Pimienta dulce
- Sweet Potato – Camote, Batata

- Yuca – Yuca, Cassava
- Zucchini – Calabacín

Poultry

- Poultry – Aves de corral
- Chicken – Pollo
- Chicken, Whole – Pollo entero
- Chechen Breast – Pechugas de pollo
- Chicken Thighs – Muslos de pollo
- Chichen Leg - Pierna de pollo
- Chicken Livers – Hígados de pollo
- Chicken Wings – Alitas de pollo
- Ground Chicken – Pollo molido
- Duck – Pato
- Eggs - Huevos
- Gizzards – Mollejas
- Turkey – Pavo
- Turkey Ham – Jamón de pavo
- Turkey Sausage – Salchicha de pavo

Beef

- Beef – Carne de vaca
- Beef, Cutlets – Carne de res, Chuletas
- Cheeseburger – Hamburguesa con queso
- Corned Beef – Carne en conserva
- Fillet of beef – Filete de ternera
- Fillet of beef – Filete de ternera
- Ground Beef – Carne molida
- Hamburger – Hamburguesa
- Meat Cubes - Cubos de carne
- Shredded Beef – Carne deshebrada

- Pork - Cerdo
- Baby Back Spare Ribs – Costillas de espalda de bebé
- Bacon – Tocino
- Boneless Sirloin – Solomillo sin hueso
- Ham – Jamón
- Ham, Smoke - Jamon ahumado
- Ham Steak – Filete de jamón
- Pigs Feet – Pies de cerdo
- Pork, Chop – Chuleta de cerdo
- Pork, Ground – Cerdo, molido
- Pork, Leg - Pierna de puerco

- Pork, Roast – Cerdo asado
- Pork, Spare Rib – Cerdo, Costilla de repuesto
- Pork Steak – Bistec de cerdo
- Pork, Tenderloin – Lomo de cerdo

- Lamb – Cordero
- Lamb, Breast – Cordero pechuga
- Lamb, Chops – Chuletas de cordero
- Lamb, Leg – Pierna de cordero
- Lamb, Ribs – Costillas de cordero
- Sheep – Oveja

Fish & Seafood

- Fish & Seafood – Pescado y mariscos
- Anchovy – Anchoa
- Caviar – Caviar
- Clam – Almeja
- Cod – Bacalao
- Crab – Cangrejo
- Eel – Anguila
- Fish – Pescado, Pez
- Herring – Arenque
- Lobster – Langosta
- Mackerel - Caballa

- Mahi-mahi – Dorado
- Mussels – Mejillones
- Octopus – Pulpo
- Oyster - ostra
- Prawn – Gamba
- Red snapper – pargo
- Salmon – Salmón
- Sardine – Sardina
- Scallop – Vieira
- Sea bass – Lubina
- Seafood or Shellfish – mariscos
- Shrimp – camarón
- Squid - Calamar
- Trout – Trucha
- Tuna – Atún
- Turbot – Rodaballo

Baking Ingredients, nuts, seeds, Grains,

- Almonds – Almendras
- Artificial sweetener - Endulzante artificial
- Baking powder – polvo para horne, Levadura en polvo
- Baking soda - Bicarbonato de sodio
- Barley – Cebada
- Bread – Pan

- Bread, sliced – Pan, rebanado
- Bread, sourdough – Pan, masa fermentada
- Bread, crumbs – Migas de pan
- Breadsticks - Palitos de pan
- Brown rice – Arroz integral
- Brown sugar – azúcar morena
- Cake – pastel
- Cane sugar – Caña de azucar
- Cashews – Anacardos
- Cereals – Cereales
- Cocoa – Cacao
- Coconut, shredded – Coco, rallado
- Confectioners sugar – Azucareros
- Crackers or cookies – galletas
- Corn – Maíz
- Cornstarch – Maicena
- Corn tortilla – Tortilla de maiz
- Cranberries, dried – Arándanos, secos
- Cream of tartar – Crema De Tartar
- Dried fruit – Fruta seca
- Flax seed – Semilla de lino
- Flour – Harina
- Flour, all-purpose - Harina para todo uso

- Flour, wheat – Harina de trigo
- Flour, whole grain – Harina de grano entero
- Hazelnut – Avellana
- Honey – Miel
- Macademia nuts – Nueces de macadamia
- Macaroni - Macarrones
- Mixed nuts – Nueces mixtas
- Noodles – Tallarines, Fideos
- Nutmeg – Nuez moscada
- Nuts – Nueces
- Oatmeal – Harina de avena
- Pasta penne – Penne pasta
- Peanuts – Mani
- Pecans – Nueces pecanas
- Pine nuts – Piñones
- Pistachio – Pistacho
- Popcorn – Palomitas de maiz
- Powder sugar – Azúcar en polvo
- Rice – Arroz

Works Sited

1. Cafasso, Jacquelyn. "Plantains: The Nutrition Facts and Health Benefits." Healthline, Healthline Media, 7 Oct. 2016, www.healthline.com/health/food-nutrition/plantain-nutrition-benefits.

2. Cynthia Sass. "7 Health Benefits of Sweet Potatoes." Health.com, 20 Feb. 2019, www.health.com/nutrition/sweet-potato-health-benefits.

3. Elliott, Brianna. "Cassava: Benefits and Dangers." Healthline, Healthline Media, 24 Mar. 2017, www.healthline.com/nutrition/cassava.

4. "Equivalents and Measures." Exploratorium, 2019, www.exploratorium.edu/cooking/convert/measurements.html.

5. Gunnars, Kris. "Top 10 Health Benefits of Eating Eggs." Healthline, Healthline Media, 28 June 2018, www.healthline.com/nutrition/10-proven-health-benefits-of-eggs.

6. Herrington, Diana. "10 Health Benefits of Mangos | Care2 Healthy Living." Healthy Living, 2019, www.care2.com/greenliving/10-health-benefits-of-mangos.html.

7. Hughes, Robert. "What Are the Benefits of Chayote?" Healthy Eating | SF Gate, 17 Dec. 2018, healthyeating.sfgate.com/benefits-chayote-7733.html.

8. Jennings, Kerri-Ann. "Top 9 Health Benefits of Eating Watermelon." Healthline, Healthline Media, 9 Aug. 2018, www.healthline.com/nutrition/watermelon-health-benefits.

9. Jha, Sameer. "11 Health Benefits of Papayas." 11 Health Benefits of Papayas, Health.India.com, 1 Mar. 2015, www.msn.com/en-in/health/nutrition/11-health-benefits-of-papayas/ar-AA2bCze.

10. LD, Megan Ware RDN. "Black Beans: Health Benefits, Facts, and Research." Medical News Today, MediLexicon International, 10 Jan. 2018, www.medicalnewstoday.com/articles/289934.php.

11. Link, Rachael. "Gut & Bone Supporter or Narcotic-Like Toxin?" Dr. Axe, 18 Dec. 2018, draxe.com/rambutan/.

12. Link, Rachael. "Soursop (Graviola): Health Benefits and Uses." Healthline, Healthline Media, 6 Oct. 2017, www.healthline.com/nutrition/soursop-benefits.

13. Meixner, Makayla. "7 Health Benefits of Dragon Fruit (Plus How to Eat It)." Healthline, Healthline Media, 23 May 2018, www.healthline.com/nutrition/dragon-fruit-benefits.

14. "Nutritionix Database." Nutritionix, 2019, www.nutritionix.com/database.

15. "Online Food Calculator. Food Volume to Weight Conversions." Online Food Calculator. Food Volume to Weight Conversions, 2019, www.aqua-calc.com/calculate/food-volume-to-weight.

16. Rodgers, Barbara. "Spotlight On The Health Benefits Of Pineapple." Barbararodgersonline.com, 15 May 2018, barbararodgersonline.com/2018/05/15/spotlight-on-the-benefits-of-pineapple/.

17. Rodgers, Barbara. "Spotlight On The Health Benefits Of Yuca." Barbararodgersonline.com, 18 Mar. 2019, barbararodgersonline.com/2019/03/18/spotlight-on-the-health-benefits-of-yuca/?fbclid=IwAR1URfmuKXRsqZyaFFbTGTjrUWGFVK6nSwydJEwhCGHYPcUXunn2KOmB0m8.

18. Spritzler, Franziska. "8 Science-Based Health Benefits of Coconut Water." Healthline, Healthline Media, 6 Sept. 2018, www.healthline.com/nutrition/8-coconut-water-benefits#section1.

19. Staughton, John. "9 Surprising Passion Fruit Benefits." Organic Facts, 6 Mar. 2019, www.organicfacts.net/health-benefits/fruit/passion-fruit.html.

20. Stewart, Martha. "Ratio of Fresh Herbs to Dry Herbs." Martha Stewart, Martha Stewart, 20 Sept. 2018, www.marthastewart.com/270213/ratio-of-fresh-herbs-to-dry-herbs.

21. "The Nutritional Value of Chicken." The National Chicken Council, 2019, www.nationalchickencouncil.org/chicken-the-preferred-protein-for-your-health-and-budget/the-nutritional-value-of-chicken/.

22. Thompson, Lisa. "Health Benefits of Raw Coconut Meat." LIVESTRONG.COM, Leaf Group, 21 Nov. 2018, www.livestrong.com/article/352244-health-nutrition-benefits-of-raw-coconut-meat/.

23. Vanovschi, Vitalii. "Nutritional Values For Common Foods And Products." Nutritional Values For Common Foods And Products, 2019, www.nutrition-value.org/.

24. Ware , Megan. "Black Beans: Health Benefits, Facts, and Research." Medical News Today, MediLexicon International, 10 Jan. 2018, www.medicalnewstoday.com/articles/289934.php.

25. Ware, Megan. "Bananas: Health Benefits, Tips, and Risks." Medical News Today, MediLexicon International, 28 Nov. 2017, www.medicalnewstoday.com/articles/271157.php.

26. Ware, Megan. "Cantaloupe: Health Benefits, Nutritional Information." Medical News Today, MediLexicon International, 15 Aug. 2017, www.medicalnewstoday.com/articles/279176.php.